Morning and Evening

by Ruth B. Esbjornson
edited by
Robert G. Esbjornson

Morning and Evening has been published with the support and encouragement of the Gustavus Adolphus College Association of Congregations; The Reverend Dennis J. Johnson, Vice President for Church Relations at Gustavus Adolphus College; Primarius Limited Publishing, Minneapolis; and friends of Ruth Esbjornson.

Copyright 1992
Gustavus Adolphus College
Saint Peter, Minnesota 56082

ISBN 0-943535-06-9

Produced in the United States of America by
Primarius Limited Publishing
Minneapolis, Minnesota 55402

FOREWORD

When my wife, Ruth, died in April 1990, I mentioned that I wanted to put together a collections of her writings for members of the family. Friends heard about my plans and asked me to make enough copies for them so I decided to publish a collection.

Ruth saved articles she had written, manuscripts of homilies and speeches she had given and many letters, so I had ample material with which to work.

In a closet, Ruth stashed away a large box of issues of *The Lutheran* in which her articles had appeared. One day in March before she died, while sitting with her in our living room as she lay on the couch, I arranged the articles by subject and date. Ruth said nothing to suggest I should reissue them; however, the fact that she saved them gave me reason to believe she would have wanted them to be accessible to others.

Most of the articles were published in *The Lutheran* in the 1960s, when Elson Ruff was editor. There were four series--*Morning and Evening*, Vol. 1, 1963; *On Being*, Vol. 2, 1964; *Jesus Said*, Vol. 3, 1965; *Hymns We Love*, Vol. 4, 1966; and several articles from later issues.

Morning and Evening is a selection of her articles from *On Being* and *Jesus Said*, combined with morning and evening prayers from the series of prayers by that title. They are arranged as morning and evening readings that could be used in various ways, particularly for personal spiritual growth.

The articles are reprinted by permission from *The Lutheran*.

Robert Esbjornson
Easter 1992

BIOGRAPHICAL NOTES

Ruth Esbjornson, born in Kinistino, Saskatchewan, May 10, 1920, was the daughter of Pastor Carl O. and Hildur [Benson] Bostrom, and was raised in Renovo, Pennsylvania; Staten Island, New York; and Braddock, Pennsylvania, places where her father was pastor in churches of the Augustana Swedish Lutheran tradition. She graduated from Gustavus Adolphus College, St. Peter, Minnesota, in 1941, and in 1945 was married to Robert Esbjornson. After five years in Newington, Connecticut, she and her husband moved to St. Peter when her husband joined the religion department of Gustavus Adolphus College. She was the mother of two children, Louise and Carl. Ruth worked in the college library for nearly 20 years until her retirement in 1982. She was a free-lance writer and regularly contributed to *The Lutheran* in the 1960s and later. As a member of First Lutheran Church in St. Peter, she was an active leader on the Church Council, in Lutheran Church Women and a member of Minnesota Synod committees. She was a regular homilist on the Christ Chapel schedule at the college and a frequent guest speaker at women's organizations and retreats. Ruth had two serious illnesses which challenged her courage and faith--diabetes for over 20 years and cancer, which was terminal. She died on April 3, 1990, just a month short of her 70th birthday.

TABLE OF CONTENTS

INTRODUCTION
Morning Prayer and Jesus Said

This collection combines the articles on sayings of Jesus with morning prayers from the *Morning and Evening* series. It can be used as a set of daily or occasional morning meditations.

Morning and Evening are prayers written in Ruth's 40s, when her children were in their active teens and I at the busiest time of my career as a college teacher. They evoke a vivid sense of spiritual responses to the common experiences of daily life. The social and secular settings become the launching pad for prayer.

On the table at Ruth's bedside after she died there was a cardboard box containing a few items often used--a comb, some bobby pins, candy (in case she needed to counteract an insulin reaction during the night) and a prayer booklet published by the Forward Movement of the Episcopal Church. She had used it so often that the pages were barely legible so she had typed three of the evening prayers on a page pasted to cardboard. She recited these every night before going to sleep. These prayers are reprinted with the last three **On Being** meditations. She had her very private praying time as well as times with the family and the congregations.

Pastor Timothy Thoresen, dean of the Minnesota Valley Conference of the Minnesota Synod of the Evangelical Lutheran Church in America at the time of Ruth's death, related the story of an encounter with Ruth on the college campus one day. In his remarks during the program after the burial service for Ruth, he commented on the relationship of private to public prayer in her life.

"Ruth was one to share her thoughts in writing. Somewhere there was a line that at one end was public and at the other end was private. Ruth moved easily between what was the public ritual of the church and the private and put words to that movement.

"I remember it as a Saturday when classes were not in session. I came around a corner and almost bumped into Ruth. She was walking with her head down, so I startled

her. She was alone and had been crying. To be interrupted in that embarrassed her. There was a bit of awkwardness in her smile as she said, 'I was just praying.' Feeling the need to explain, she said, 'I do this often.' She found the most private place, out there in the open. And there she did what is most private--she cried--as we do--she went home from that probably refreshed in body and soul.

"I thought of that on my way home that day. What a wonderful model. Prayer is private and we will hear it also later in public."

In our shared times of prayer, her petitions and intercessions often ended with a sardonic little laugh, as if to say, "Who am I to expect God to grant my requests or even hear them?" Her faith was a blend of skepticism and hope, confidence and uncertainty, but yet enlivened by a sense of God's presence and centered in Jesus Christ.

Ruth expressed her understanding of prayer in this excerpt from an article entitled "What Do You Pray For?" [***The Lutheran***, January 4, 1967]:

Prayer should be the irresistible urge to come into the presence of one who is holy, good, obedient, pure and strong enough to sweep you out of yourself. It is Jesus who should occupy your thoughts, not yourself.

This insight was underscored later by experiences of praying with the Benedictine monks at the abbey church on the campus of St. John's University in Collegeville, Minnesota. I had a sabbatical in 1973, four months of which were at the Institute of Ecumenical and Cultural Research. At the beginning of our time there, we made a decision to go regularly to the morning and evening prayers at the abbey church. It turned out to be one of the important decisions of our lives because it transformed our life-style and enriched our praying practices. The benefits that came from the decision were unplanned and unexpected.

The Benedictine prayer offices are done in a deliberate manner characteristic of a disciplined life. The monks come in silently, wait in silence or in meditation for the first hymn. They sit in choir stalls on either side of the chancel, the center of which is the altar. At every service they recite or chant psalms antiphonally, alternating between the two choirs. Between each psalm there is about a minute for silent meditation. Then there is a reading from Scripture or some other ancient, medieval or modern source as well. One of the monks leads the brief prayers of petition and intercession and of remembrance of those that have gone to their eternal home. The service ends with the Lord's Prayer and the abbot's blessing. This goes on day after day. When all the psalms have been used, the monks begin all over again.

One day it occurred to me that Benedictines have been praying like this for about 1500 years, and they would be praying this way daily after we returned home and after we were dead and perhaps for many centuries. We were stepping into a long, long story of prayer and worship that linked them and now us to God. I thought about the steady pulse of the Atlantic Ocean's surf, its breakers crashing rhythmically onto the sand of Nauset Beach--swish . . . swish . . . swish--a sound that has gone on for thousands of years and will continue for eons more, before and after our vacation times there.

Now I heard and sang the psalms as the steady pulse of prayer, going on all my life and in churches and monasteries and convents all over the world. The steady rhythms of prayer, when we enter them consciously and regularly, become conscious, and so we become aware that our lives are linked to a greater story than our own, to the story of God's people and to God's life.

We brought that new consciousness back home and altered our prayer practices. Ruth and I had morning prayer after breakfast in our later years--a combination of reading, conversation and praying. After breakfast, we sat on the couch where we could watch the dawn come through the large window opening to the east. We began with the morning litany on page 162 of the *Lutheran Book of Worship*, "O God, we cry to you for help. In the morning our prayer comes before you . . . ." We sang a hymn, sometimes chanted a psalm; we read a passage from the Bible and then each of us read from a modern book we had chosen. Our prayers were a conversation between us and before the presence of God about all sorts of situations facing us and about people we cared for. We ended with morning prayer on page 163 of the **Lutheran Book of Worship** and the Lord's Prayer.

This regular practice became as important to us as eating or exercising. We were able to do so at that time in our lives [after children had left home] when the pace of life had become a bit slower. Our prayer life before that time was pretty much confined to very brief devotions as a family, church settings and in our private times.

In those times together, we realized more and more that praying was a matter of being present to God, paying attention to God in silence, in the Word of Scripture and the Word coming through others as well. Prayer was not so much pleading for God's attention as paying attention to God. We lived a praying life, both of us, all our lives, that is life lived in the presence of God in whom we live and move and have our being. Praying is not just saying prayers; it is a matter of living prayerfully.

The *Jesus Said* articles are personal reflections on words attributed to Jesus. They are not exegetical studies. Many of the sayings of Jesus troubled Ruth, but she consistently affirmed the central place of Jesus Christ in her working faith nevertheless. This ambivalent attitude is evident in an excerpt from one of her sermons.

>   *Jesus has the capacity to make me more uncomfortable than anyone in my life. There is a statement I see on the bumpers of cars: 'Jesus is the Answer.' What does it mean? Just cry out or shout 'Jesus!' and all problems are solved? I heard a man who appalled me one Sunday morning on television.*
>
>   *He sat in a comfortable chair, decked in fashionable garb, obviously hale, hearty, and well fed and said, 'I am a happy man,' and grinned. 'I never worry. Jesus does everything for me. Jesus died for my sins. Jesus takes all my cares on him. And since I have accepted Jesus I am a free man, free of worry or care about anything or anyone.'*

Now obviously he has not read the words of this man Jesus in the Bible he was patting so fondly with his hand. Jesus said things like 'take my cross upon you . . . Unless you care for those in prison, without food or shelter, those who are sick, you do not care for me.' Jesus said things that make it impossible for me to accept all the good things I have, including this lovely church, this good coffee and cake, my warm house, without feeling a sense of responsibility for all those who do not have these things. In the church we are never free of concern, never free of demands. It is true Jesus has given us the greatest gift a person can receive, but it is also true that Jesus makes demands, very hard demands.

However, nothing I have ever heard even comes close to the understanding Jesus had of the human condition or of the deep and abiding love without which life has little to offer in the way of meaning. The thought of Jesus is so profound and yet at the same time so simple that no other person, it seems to me, has ever matched him in wisdom. The study of the Bible becomes more intriguing the more one attempts to plumb its depths.

WHAT DO YOU PRAY FOR?

JESUS SAID:
Daughter, your faith has made you well. Go in peace.

It is the middle of the night. You have wakened feeling sick. So often you feel sick. It is so dreary feeling this way so often. If only it would all end. Is there something wrong with you?

All that the woman to whom Jesus spoke these words had done was to touch the hem of his robe and he made her well. You have prayed many times to Jesus. You have cried to him but you are still sick. What is wrong with your prayers?

Let's analyze it.

What is it that makes you turn to Jesus? Is it your discomfort? Is it your desire to be well? Do you go to him because you want things to be better than they are?

Let's look at the woman whom Jesus calls "Daughter." She is in a large crowd of people around him. She is moved by this man. And because she is drawn to him, she quickly and unobtrusively touches the hem of his garment--not to attract his attention to herself but just that she might have a single moment when she can be identified with him.

And in all that crowd Jesus knows that someone has touched him in awe and reverence, someone has communicated with him.

This woman was attracted to Jesus. She wanted to get near him. She wanted to be a part of him by touching him.

She was not trying to make Jesus come to her. She was not trying to make Jesus pay attention to her. She went to him. He was at the center of her thoughts. In that moment she became well because for once she was drawn outside herself to give her thoughts wholeheartedly to someone else.

Her faith had become single-hearted. It had become centered on Jesus.

Do you pray to Jesus because you cannot resist him? Do you pray to him because you want to be in his presence? Do you pray to him because you want to communicate with him?

Or do you pray because you want something from him? Or because, if nothing else works, maybe this will, or because you've been a church member all your life and you ought to get some good out of it?

Prayer should be the irresistible urge to come into the presence of One who is holy, good, obedient, pure, and strong enough to sweep you out of yourself. It is Jesus who should occupy your thoughts, not yourself.

Faith in this man is a faith that draws your thoughts to God like a mighty magnet pulling all the bobby pins out of your hair. It pulls your thoughts beyond the confines of yourself. This is the faith that can make you a whole person, maybe not always a healthy one, but always a whole one.

"Forgive me, Lord, for being so self-centered and small. I know that I should keep you in sight no matter how big the crowd is. If I weren't thinking about myself so often, I'd never lose sight of you, but I do. If I'd keep you in my mind's eyes, I could probably even touch the hem of your garment. What a day that would be! Let me not be out of the crowd around you when it comes. Amen."

MORNING PRAYER

Some mornings I wake up uncheerfully.

My back aches or my head feels tight or I feel stiff and unrelaxed. That joyful new feeling that makes the birds sing, roosters crow, and little children jump eagerly up and down in their beds is not there.

Yet one thing does make me joyful, even though I might not be exuberant.

I am awake. I know that it is day. I see the light. I can move out of my bed. My mind is functioning. I have something to do. I am aware of my surroundings, my feelings and my thoughts. For this I am glad.

"Oh God, I thank thee for this morning. Help me to improve my disposition as the day goes by. There are good things to this day. Let me find them. Let me dwell on them. Help me to cope with the dreary things that may occur. In Jesus' name. Amen."

JESUS SAID:
Beware of false prophets, who come to you in sheep's clothing, but inwardly they are ravening wolves.
- Matthew 7:15

He is standing in his attic. He is dreaming about being a painter. The attic has a big window facing north. He sees where he could set an easel.

Even as he is standing there, his wife's voice comes up, reminding him of an appointment. She is indeed his helpmate, reminding him constantly of appointments to be kept, meetings to be attended, clients to be hosted, people to be entertained. Her life seems to be spent in constant service to his advancement.

He walks slowly down the stairs from the attic.

The telephone rings. No one answers. It rings again. Mother, her hands covered with flour, picks it up.

It's for her teen-age daughter--a boy's voice. The mother smiles contentedly. Already her daughter has boys calling. The braces, the charm school, the investment in clothes are paying off. She need not be silent when other mothers describe their daughters' popularity.

"It's for you," she calls to her daughter who is lying on her bed completely lost in a book.

The girl lays the book aside and goes downstairs.

When she hears who it is, she wants to slam down the receiver, but she doesn't. Her mother is there. She is always telling her how lucky she is to be popular, how important it is to cultivate people, particularly boys. But she honestly doesn't care for boys yet. She'd like to be left alone. But her mother pushes her all the time.

He slumps into a huge, cushioned chair. His feet are propped on a footstool. He is reading a journal. His body is resting, but not his mind. It is churning with ideas stirred by the article. These ideas will gestate, later to be born through the pain of sermon preparation.

But the doorbell rings. It is the postman.

The pastor takes the mail. He opens it. It is full of reminders of meetings to be attended, projects to be started, reports to be filled in. He might as well begin.

The journal slips off the arm of the chair to the floor, the place of reading is lost, never to be resumed.

Wives, mothers, the church--all good things. But in these cases they take the form of the good thing, yet actually for these people they are like wolves, consuming rather than enriching the person.

It is easy to recognize evil when it has an evil form. It is when evil has disguised itself as the good that it is hard to combat. Sometimes ambition is a good thing, sometimes it is evil.

The wife, the mother, the church were all ambitious for another, but they were all arrogant. They felt they knew what was best, but maybe God had planted in these people other desires, other fits that should be nurtured. To demand too much of another can give to each of us the character of a wolf.

It would be wise to heed Jesus' words and to look at ourselves not only as people who need to beware of wolves disguised as sheep who might be using us, but to look to ourselves to be sure that we have not become wolves that are consuming other people.

"Dear Lord, grant me understanding so that I may recognize the wolf in myself as well as the wolf in others. Amen."

MORNING PRAYER

Day is at hand.

I must rise up from this cozy bed, this languid pose, and move about with cheerful energy. I wonder if I can do it. I turn over again and bury my face in my pillow. Come, come, the day is waiting. Be idle no longer, my mind declares to me sternly.

Ah! But I have something I must do first

I forget my bed, my desires, my future tasks. My mind keeps still so that I can pray

"Eternal Father, who hast given me the night of rest now past, bend thine ear to hear me. I want to thank thee for thy endless love that hast brought me to the desire to pray to thee, to want thy presence in my life. Be with me and those I love this day. In Jesus' name. Amen."

JESUS SAID:
He who has ears to hear, let him hear.

- Luke 8:8

Why do some people sense God when they hear a mighty sound of music, when they see a meadowlark fly by their window, when they feel the ocean's salty spray, when they experience a nurse's soothing touch, when they read a mathematical formula, when they hear a psalm in church, when they open the Bible?

Why do some people never sense God though "The Messiah" thunders in their ears, though they fly in a powerful jet at 29,000 feet above the earth, though their bodies surge with health as they ride the surf at Waikiki, though their libraries are filled with books where men attempt by poetry or philosophy or theology to describe the mystery and the mighty acts of God, though they hear the impressive words of the Bible at wedding or baptism or funeral services?

Is it because some have been given spiritual ears and some have not?

That hardly seems fair. That hardly seems God-like. For though we are all created with individual differences, with individual abilities, surely we are all created with the possibility of hearing God speak.

Here is a person who loves to walk through the northern woods alone on an autumn day. The leaves crunch under his feet. He breathes the tangy air. He hears the lone cry of a bird. He loves the vast stillness. Creation cries aloud to him of the glory of God at such a moment.

Here is another person who loves to join the crowds in a football stadium. He shouts greetings to his friends. He leaps to his feet in a tense moment. He is exhilarated when his team makes a touchdown. Life to him is like a great game with God calling the plays.

It would be foolish to expect the football-loving man to find God in the northern woods if he hates the northern woods. It would be foolish to expect the quiet man to find God at a football game if he hates crowds. But actually God can be meaningful to each man in his particular interest. God is restricted to neither.

To the poet, God springs to life in mysterious images that paint themselves on his mind. To the abstract thinker, God can be found worthy of worship in the complexities of the mathematical formula. God is restricted to neither.

Each man must find God in his own way and no man must demand that another man find God in just the way he does. Christians have sometimes made the mistake of demanding of every man that God come in exactly the same way he came to them. This is unreasonable, sectarian.

But how, then, can a man know if he has truly found God? For there is a way in which all men may come to God regardless of individual differences or abilities. There is one way God speaks that all men may understand.

It is in our response to Jesus. If we sense when we hear the words of Jesus that what he says is truth, then we have truly found God--no matter in what place in life we express it. But if we cannot find him in Christ, then our spiritual ears are deaf no matter how glorious seems creation, or how great the football game, or how moving the poem or how abstract the formula.

It is when we hear Christ speak to us that everything else we enjoy takes on new meaning and new depth. He comes to flash light into the dark depths of our soul. He comes to unlock that locked door in our minds. He comes to breathe love into those dry, dusty lungs.

"Forgive me, Lord, when I have refused to hear your words, when I have refused to understand their meaning for me. Let my ears open up so that hearing I might act, and acting I might live. Amen."

MORNING PRAYER

This morning I slept so long there are others up before me. The house is crackling with activity. Doors are opening and closing. Dishes and silver are clanging. I must hurry to meet the demands of the day. I can't linger here for philosophical thoughts or imaginative ideas. Action is the word.

But I must take time to pray.

"Oh God, who canst put energy into my body, give me enormous capacity for giving out joy and radiance to those about me. Give me the will to work and the desire to please thee as well as others. Help me to smile, Lord, as I hurry to my tasks. In Jesus' name. Amen."

JESUS SAID:

So they are no longer two but one. What therefore God has joined together, let no man put asunder.

- Matthew 19:6

You know how if feels to be hungry. Your mouth is dry. Your stomach feels like an empty pit. You walk by a fruit stand. Pears, bananas, oranges, cherries, peaches and apples are all displayed before you.

"Try one of these apples. They're new," the fruit man says.

You take the hard red apple gratefully. The sweet but tangy juice is absorbed by your taste buds. You crush the hard, firm flesh of the apple in your teeth. It is a moment of gustatory bliss.

You find out from the fruit man that this taste-satisfying apple is the result of a new graft. Two varieties of apples were grafted to produce a new apple. When the graft takes, when the two strains merge, a whole new tree is created. It is a tree that bears new fruit.

Marriage is just such a graft. Two personalities are grafted to become one new personality. According to Jesus, God has made the man and the woman to complement each other, to become one new person.

This is the secret of Christian marriage. No Christian should go into marriage hoping to cling to his own individuality so that he may continually assert it. A Christian goes into marriage knowing that here God is creating something new, just as he once created you from that bit of protoplasm you once were.

Now he is taking two distinct individuals, each with some good traits, to merge them into one unit. Together this should create a better unit than each single unit was before. This unit should become so much more creative, more productive and more complete that the individual no longer feels like an individual without the other one.

Actually this is the basic unit in society, this foundation upon which the family is laid.

This is the reason no Christian should marry without a clear understanding of what marriage is. When he considers marrying someone, he should think to himself, "Is this the person for whom I am willing to give up my own personality, my own individuality? Is this the person with whom I want to create a new personality?"

Unless this is true, the marriage will not be what God intended it to be--a new creation. Instead it will detract from the individual, for where the new branches were intended to be grafted when the marriage vows were taken, there will be only blank places on the tree. The tree must be willing to accept the new graft to become a new tree with the possibility of new fruit.

It is also the reason why the Christian can hardly ever find the true nature of marriage unless he also marries a Christian, for the grafting of unlike trees is difficult to achieve. Usually the tree will fail to accept the graft, and it will be a misshapen tree.

This is why, I think, that Jesus seemed to consider the question of divorce almost irrelevant--for a truly God-created marriage has created one personality out of two. There is nothing left to divorce. There are not two people to divide.

The Christian needs to understand what marriage is before he enters that state, for then divorce becomes an impossibility. And in marriage the new personality has to grow and mature with all the aches, pains and mistakes of any growing personality. But it is a growing, living, throbbing, meaningful state that truly enriches life.

"Forgive me, Lord, for sometimes resisting the rewarding creation that you intended my marriage to be when my will needed to be blended with another's. And thank you, Lord, for making the delightful institution of marriage to carry out your plans for mankind. Amen."

MORNING PRAYER

Morning "breaks."

I wonder who thought of that word? Morning doesn't "break." There is no loud crashing noise. There are no broken pieces. No one is hurling something through space.

Morning slips over the earth so quietly one can easily miss its coming. All at once it is here, the beginning of a new day. This day is as fresh as a new house that gleams with a satin finish--no sagging steps, no fingerprints, no worn spots--just ready to step into. There are possibilities in this day.

I want to know them and to use them, so I pray.

"Dear God, give me a desire to do the tasks I have this day, even those same dull ones I have every day. Let me think of new ways to do some of the old ones. Let me not think so much of the tasks I have to do but rather of the people I have to serve. In Jesus' name. Amen."

JESUS SAID:

You are the salt of the earth; but if salt has lost its taste, how shall its saltness be restored? It is no longer good for anything except to be thrown out and trodden under foot by men.

- Matthew 5:13

Do you like to eat?

Do you like potato chips, peanuts, crackers and cheese? Do you like hamburgers off the grill, steaks still sputtering in hot fat and juice, a fresh trout with a dash of lemon?

But what would any of these be without salt? The same food value but not the same taste.

Jesus said that we are the salt of the earth. What a delightful comparison!

We are the people who give life its zest, its charm, its flavor of life. We find the tantalizing something that makes life more than a dull and tasteless routine. We make life a luxury in which we can find pleasure.

Are you able to do that with your life?

Are you able to season it with enough Christianity to be able to taste life with a gourmet's satisfaction in something truly good? Is your Christianity the kind that brings into your life a tang, a zest, a taste for its goodness?

Or is it a drag on you, a strained effort at being good, a depressing duty that pulls you to worship on Sunday and steals money out of your wallet for the offering?

If it is, that's not Christianity that you've been subscribing to all these years. That might be some kind of religion, but it's not Christianity. Christianity is a salt. Christianity is what gives life its zing, its extra something, its taste.

But as Jesus says, salt can lose its taste. Maybe that has happened to you as a Christian. Maybe the faith of Jesus, the glow of worship, the intellectual exercise of having your mind work as you read the Bible, the satisfaction of being concerned over the needs of others, the mystical sense of God's holiness--maybe this has gone from your life. Maybe the true flavor of the salt is all gone.

Maybe this happens to the church at times just as it happens to you. Maybe this is why the church and Christians are sometimes trodden under foot and ignored.

What a pity! How far from what Jesus intended! How tasteless life is under those circumstances!

There is salt to be had. Jesus supplies the salt, the flavoring to life. Jesus does not supply salt to just one small area of life, to those whose occupation is work in the church. He can supply it everywhere--in art, music, drama, literature, the wilderness, in people everywhere.

Jesus is the one who adds flavor to every vocation. He brings the flavor to every way of life.

He brings it through the church. So the church has to be filled with salty Christians who are willing to sprinkle salt wherever they go.

The church must be concerned and ready to enter into every area of life--politics, education, vocation, culture, health and recreation. It wants to bring zest and flavor to all these activities--not an artificial flavor, but the real thing.

See if you can't lick your lips and get set to taste that salty goodness again, the goodness of a life in Christ.

"Dear Lord, renew a right spirit within us so that we may bring happiness and understanding and inspiration to others. Help us to see the joy and peace that your blessed presence brings and to reflect it by being bringers of gladness and makers of peace wherever we go. Amen."

MORNING PRAYER

It is light again.

I can see all the things that were hidden during the night - my room, the pictures of my family, my books. It is wonderful to awaken in this familiar place.

But I can also see the dust under my desk, the papers on top of it, the clothes on the chair, and I know what I will see in the rest of the house.

There are many things to be done, little jobs that will keep me moving most of the day.

I could be irritated by these trivial jobs so that by the end of the day I am one great irritation to everyone around me.

Or I could be pleased with the fact that everything looks better when I am done, that it is a relatively easy job, that no one is telling me what to do, that I can listen to good music as I work. I can think and I can pray.

"Dear Lord, help me to be pleasant and grateful this day. Help me to be energetic. Help me to see little things in perspective. In Jesus' name. Amen."

JESUS SAID:
The Father judges no one, but has given all judgment to the Son.
- John 5:22

Her mind was full of thoughts. So she wrote a poem. But it wasn't enough to write a poem. Someone had to read it. Naturally her husband was the obvious choice. He read it. "Why, darling, this is wonderful. I didn't know I had such a talented wife."

She felt all warm inside at his praise. She decided to use that poem when she gave the devotions at her next group meeting.

"I didn't know you were a poet," her friends exclaimed.

Elated, she sent it to an editor. But it came back judged inadequate for publishing.

A man felt the need to express himself. He got some oils, canvas and brushes.

He painted a picture. It was better than he thought it would be so he showed it to his wife.

"To think that I've been married to an artist all these years!" She hugged him. He felt flattered when she had it framed and hung on their wall.

Their friends were amazed. Why not enter it in the local art show?

Three competent artists made a judgment of the entries. No mention was made of his.

Under qualified judges, neither the man nor the woman was truly a poet or an artist even though others thought so.

There are many people who feel that they are qualified to make moral judgments. They make judgments about the society in which they live; they make judgments about their neighbors. They make judgments based on their own limited experience and viewpoint.

And their judgments mislead people upon whom they make them. The teen-ager listens to the judgment of his peers, the employee to the judgment of his boss, the matron to the judgment of her society. Now it is possible for these people to make judgments on certain matters, matters on which they are qualified to make judgment.

But there is only one Person qualified to make moral judgment. He is the only one so obedient to God that there is in him no rebellion against God, no defiance toward God, no hatred for God, no indifference to God, no hiding from God. He is so in harmony with God that God trusts him completely. It is when our deeds come under his scrutiny that qualified judgment is made of our moral behavior not under anyone else's judgment. Frequently the judgment of others seems mild compared to his. But he alone sits as Judge.

When he does, the selfish things we do so carefully concealed from others, sometimes even from ourselves stand out like ugly scars on a freshly scrubbed face.

The lies we tell, so artfully clothed in polite language suddenly scream aloud their falseness.

The sensual and erotic dreams that we deliberately revel in are exposed as the frankly lustful pictures they are.

The hopes we have that others may fail so we may succeed show us how malicious we can be.

Morality is a word that is flung about with great abandon. But no one should dare use the word who is not also willing to have what he believes to be morality come under the judgment of Jesus Christ. It is here that the word takes on meaning, that it takes on depth, that it becomes clarified. For God makes no moral judgments except through Jesus Christ.

"Forgive me, Lord, when I think myself able to sit in moral judgment of others. Let me, instead, exhibit my behavior to thy sight and welcome thy judgment on my life. And then I know I will have to cast myself upon thy forgiving love. Amen."

MORNING PRAYER

I open my eyes to a new day.

I want to wake up eagerly. I want to be cheerful with my family, my friends, my associates. But I feel strangely weary. I remember other mornings when I have awakened with eagerness only to fill my day with mistakes, angry words and frustrating experiences.

Will that happen again?

It might--but it might not. I have hope--hope, like the sun rising each morning in my mind. I have God.

"Oh God, awaken in me the joy at being alive to begin another day. Fill me with desire to be loving and kind in my attitudes toward others. Help me to find in my work a fulfillment of the purpose for which I was born. For Jesus' sake. Amen."

JESUS SAID:
Why are you afraid, O men of little faith?

- Matthew 8:26

There are moments in my life of which I am not proud.

It is the moment of the countdown when a man is to be blasted into space 10-9-8-7-6-5-. I run from the room where the TV is showing the event before the great moment.

The pressure has built up in me to such an extent that I cannot stand to see what will happen. It might be something terrible. Instead of being excited, instead of being thrilled at the possibilities of new sights, new experiences, and new worlds for man to possess, I let dread capture my senses.

It is the moment in the motion picture when a man is going to take a leap across the crevasse in the mountains. I see the dark depths and the icy walls. I feel the shuddering sensation of the slip and the plunge into space. I close my eyes. I cannot look.

"Tell me when he made it," I whisper as I nudge my husband. Instead of entering into this grave but glorious moment in the life of a man when he stakes his life on his ability to surmount difficulty, when he dares to do the difficult, when he shows the glory of being a man, I let that moment be lost instead to a feeling of dread and of fear.

It is the night before a family vacation trip. I lie in my bed thinking how snug we are in our little house, what pleasant moments we have together in our neighborhood, what interesting things occur on our college campus. Why leave it? Why take a chance out on those travel-clogged highways? Why go to those cities packed with people and turbulence? Instead of being grateful for the chance to see new people, to see new sights, to widen my horizons, I am numbed by this morbid anxiety.

Jesus is trying to shake people like me loose from those strangling ropes of fear. He knew that life had wonderful possibilities for men. He knew that a man is largely what he believes. It is the man who believes he can do something, that he can be something, that he can find something, who does it.

Jesus shows what a man who has faith can do. Jesus has shown better than any other man what faith can do. Jesus believed that he was the Son of God. Jesus believed that his Father spoke to him. Jesus believed that God could show his love to man through him. Even when he hung on the cross, when most men would have given up the whole idea, he clung tenaciously to this belief that he was the son of his Father.

And he was.

Belief in the ability to do something becomes a fact when it has been accomplished. It is no longer belief then, but fact.

It is no longer a belief that man can go into space. It is a fact.

It is no longer a belief that a man has climbed a mountain after he has done it. It is a fact.

It is no longer a belief that one can take a stimulating vacation after he has. It is a fact.

But faith is a necessary ingredient to accomplishment, the ability to believe that one can.

Faith is the glorious requirement of the Christian commitment-- the faith that God, through Jesus, can redeem a man, even a fearful one like me.

And one day this belief becomes a fact.

"Oh Lord, forgive me those fearful moments that I keep dreaming up in my life. Let me, instead, be filled with the excitement of faith, of believing in something good, something tremendous, something glorious, a life filled with expectation rather than dread. Amen."

MORNING PRAYER

It is so quiet. What woke me? There is no one stirring. The alarm has not rung. But the morning is here.

Is there something in me that does not sleep, that keeps me awake? Just think! There is a part of me that keeps on going even when I am fast asleep. Such an amazing creature I really am!

How grateful I should be for what I am, not for any worthiness in me, but because God made me to be such an intricate, delicate, precious human being--for to be human is something precious.

"Oh God, I thank thee for making me and all those I love. I thank thee most of all for having made us human beings because thou didst desire to love us. In Jesus' name. Amen."

JESUS SAID:
Fear not, therefore; you are of more value than many sparrows.

- Matthew 10:31

I stood by my window watching the snow come down. The wind was howling and the snow was beginning to look like great white sheets billowing wildly back and forth.

The next day drifts of snow 20 feet high had turned our flat backyard into a mountain range with hills and valleys for the children to slither up and slide down.

I had read somewhere that each snowflake has its own pattern and its own identity. No two are alike.

Frankly, I could not believe it. When I looked out and saw the billions of flakes it must have taken to make those mountains of snow, my mind was incapable of imagining that many different, tiny, flaky patterns.

Such are the limits of my mind.

I have the same difficulty when I ride a subway at the rush hour, when I see the hordes of people leaving a baseball game, when I sit on my little square of sand on the beach on a hot, summer day while endless children run by. The world is just littered with people.

Yet all these people are individuals. Each is a different person. No two are alike. Each is know to God.

"No," I say to myself. "That is impossible. How could anyone know, love and care for each of these persons with the kind of love I hope God has for me?"

But I have seen the snowflakes. I have shoveled them, I have slid on them, I have even tasted them. I know they were there.

Jesus, being in a different climate, talks about sparrows rather than snowflakes. But his point is that each one was created by design, each one is known by its creator.

And each human being is created by design. Each one has value. Each person is worthy of God's attention.

Though my mind is incapable of conceiving such love, such creativity, such glory, that does not mean that it does not exist.

Jesus was capable of understanding that kind of love. He could grasp the immense creative power of God. He could, with confidence, say that God is capable of knowing and loving each person born.

Since my love could not stand that kind of strain, since my brain is limited, since my emotional capacity is drained just thinking about it, it is necessary that I have a source to which I continually go to be revived. Since there is not much I can claim to be--the lover of so few people, the creator of so little, only one tiny flake in those billions created--I must go somewhere to get the feeling of worth that a human being needs to possess. I need to find someone bigger than I am, greater than I am, more loving than I am, to satisfy this longing to have an existence that is meaningful.

Jesus says that what I need is God. God is the one who can supply me with worth, for in contact with God I can partake of the greatness that can create a universe, a love that can warm each living soul, and a goodness that, like water gushing from a fountain, can wash the dirt that clogs those streets in my brain. It is when I think of such a God that joy bubbles in my consciousness, warmth radiates through my senses and dignity straightens my back.

Jesus says that the fact of God is not a dream; it is not a wish, it is not a fanciful thought. It is a reality.

My sadness over the human predicament, my inability to find meaning within myself, my failure to be truly good, my confusion over the complexity of modern society--all can be dispelled when I contemplate the God revealed in Jesus who through these many years has been the great source of comfort, the true author of life, and the real Savior of each man who turns to him.

"Thank you, Lord."

MORNING PRAYER

The sun is streaming through the edges around the shade drawn over my window. It sends streaks of light quivering on the walls of my room. I lie here watching the light shimmer in elongated patterns. I marvel at the beauty of so small a thing.

It makes me think of other lovely things I see during the day--the pine trees from my kitchen window, the bowl of oranges on the table, the twinkle in my husband's eyes when he teases me, the glow in my children's cheeks when they burst into the house.

"For these and many other things that I see and hear daily, I thank thee, Oh Lord. Forgive me when I grumble about what I do not have. Help me to be grateful. In Jesus' name. Amen."

JESUS SAID:
Blessed are the poor in spirit, for theirs is the kingdom of heaven.

- Matthew 5:3

It is a late winter afternoon. The sun has already dipped out of sight leaving a pale gray sky. A man is walking home. It is very quiet. He can hear his feet crunching on the snow. He is tired. He wants to get home but at the same time he feels too weary to shout gaily to his wife or to listen to the strident voices of his children wanting to tell him what they have done this day.

He feels poor in spirit. His energy is not boundless. He is no conqueror of difficulties. He is a very ordinary man subject to weariness and to uncertainty.

But because he knows that he is a simple man, because he feels that he cannot make his own destiny, because he longs to find a resource greater than himself, he prays. He confronts God on this walk home in this quiet evening. He empties himself of his human pride, his human desire to be important and his human desire to be an infallible parent. But he is not yet standing before God with empty hands for they are still full of tiredness. So he pours all that weariness out before God, too.

Now that he has thrown away those cumbersome weights, he forgets himself and concentrates on God, the God who penciled in those black branches against a gray sky, the God whose spirit soars beyond that evening star, the God who gave him that waiting family, the God who even now touches him with a sense of the holy.

This man that was empty begins to get filled. There is something with which God invariably fills human beings who turn to him to empty themselves before him. He pours his love into them and this love is what transforms the life of any man. So the man finishes his walk home a new man--no longer poor, for he has inherited a kingdom.

But he could never have inherited this kingdom had he not first been poor in spirit, so poor that he needed to find help. It is the poor who have to seek riches if they are to fulfill their desires.

It is the poor in spirit who need to find the eternal Spirit from which they can draw. It is the man who knows that he is poor who turns to God. It is the poor man who will listen to what God has to say to him. The poor man will not look into himself to find what he should do, for he knows that there isn't much there.

Jesus here is not speaking in terms of economics. Poverty is hardly a blessed state.

Jesus is speaking of the poor in spirit to whom pride is a negative attribute. The man who dares God to prove his existence, the man who demands of God proof of his mercy, the man who mimics God in ribald satire, the man who defies God in unlawful acts, is a proud man, a man of haughty spirit. He will never find God, for that is not the kind of person God is.

It is the man who goes to God because he knows that he needs him, because he knows that he cannot live without him, because he knows that he must claim his spirit since he has none of his own, who inherits this kingdom of love, mercy and holiness.

Jesus says that such a person is happy--not happy in the sense of the child whose hand clutches the nickel with which he can buy a candy bar, but happy in the sense of the child who has been forlornly lost in the crowd who suddenly comes alive with happiness because he has found his mother. For in God he finds the Spirit for which his spirit longs. God is what makes existence bearable and heaven desirable.

"Forgive me, Lord, for the pride that makes me stubborn and that makes my legs stiffen when they should bend before thee. I am the loser, I know. And I acknowledge now my need for thee and my desire for thee. Amen."

MORNING PRAYER

I hear the morning come before I see it--a bird calling, the truck chugging down the highway, the paperboy as he slams my front door, the creak of a bedspring as one of my family stirs.

How many sounds there are in the world!

Most of them I never hear. I'm sorry I miss some of them. I'm sure my life would be richer if I listened for some of the things I don't hear--the swishing wind as it blows across the prairie behind my house has music all its own; the words of my children delight me when I listen to what they say--it annoys me when I only hear the chatter of their voices punctuated by high-pitched squeaks; the typing of my husband's typewriter--when I only hear its clatter I could scream, but when I really listen, I catch the rhythm of a mind at work.

"Dear God, help me to listen this day to the things to which I usually give little heed. Let me hear the whispers as well as the shouts. For Jesus' sake. Amen."

JESUS SAID:

If they do not hear Moses and the prophets, neither will they be convinced if some one should rise from the dead.

- Luke 16:31

Magicians sometimes make us gasp with surprise as they reveal their dexterity.

A séance might cause us to delve into interesting speculations about the possibilities of the spirit world.

The use of a new drug that caused rapid recovery from a devastating illness makes us thankful to God for the moment.

We are intrigued at having our prosaic little world shaken. It excites us momentarily to see something different, to have the usual, visible world challenged, and to have our credulity jolted.

Our senses respond to the excitement of the moment. But the stimulation does not last. Once we are back in our common routines, we are as we were--puttering along at our usual pace.

This is just what Jesus is interested in--our usual routines, our every-day patterns, our common attitudes. This is where he wants his influence to take effect. He knows this is where it counts. He has to become a part of our being.

Jesus is not interested in creating a sensation, in providing a momentary thrill, in giving a shot in the arm, in arousing our wonder at a bizarre happening. Jesus knows that what matters is how we think, how we act, how we respond to ordinary situations. Our lives must be God-centered every day.

People who respond to Jesus because they see a miracle of healing, or because someone uses Jesus' words as a philosophy for starting a new peace movement, or because some of Jesus' ideas create a sensation that results in good business climate are not followers of Jesus. All these things might result from taking Jesus seriously, but they are only a small part of what Jesus wants and intends for us.

Men are not apt to change their attitudes because of one exciting, earth-shaking happening. A change in attitudes or one's thinking patterns is usually the result of a slow infiltration, a gradual growth.

Jesus wants men's souls "for keeps." He wants the world to know him through people who are consistently different, whose lives reveal love, purity, reverence for the holy and mercy toward all men.

Christians have sometimes fallen for the idea of making the church sensational through a variety of gimmicks, but it is not Jesus' way.

Jesus' way is much harder. His is a daily revealing of his life and his love in the people who follow him--faithful attendance at worship to reveal their reverence for the holy, willing service in the community to show their compassion toward others, a consistent attitude of honesty, justice and truthfulness to show their belief in the purity of lives dedicated to Christ, and a persistent holding to love as the guiding motivation for their lives. This is how Jesus wants to persuade people to follow him.

Nothing miraculous has to happen to lure men to God. No sensational episode has to drug them into seeing God in the fantastic. To people who truly love God each day, life itself is the miracle. Sensational acts of magic, the emotional impact of that spirit world, and even the wonderful potency of the new drugs create sensations that are only minor to that one tremendous, powerful fact that God can work through them and in them his love day after day.

"Forgive me, Lord, for not always acting like a follower of thine - for wanting thy greatness to be shown by someone other than me, for wanting some exciting event to make men come to thee in throngs. Yet it is through me and all those others like me who have known thy love who must show it to others. It is a task that knows no ending and no surpassing. Amen."

MORNING PRAYER

I am one among millions of people waking just now.

I am not alone. I am a part of the human race. I work; so do others. I cry; so do others. I suffer; so do others.

These are things that I share with every mortal being.

I pray; this is something I do not share with all people. Not everyone prays, not everyone is conscious of thee, but there are enough who do pray to know that it is a fellowship of which I want to be a part, that part of the human race who seeks to know thee, to serve thee, to love thee.

"Oh God, be near me this day in all I do. Even though I am not conscious of it, let thy presence permeate my being so that I cannot exist apart from thee any more than I can exist apart from the air I breathe. In Jesus' name. Amen."

JESUS SAID:

You are the rock, and on this rock I will build my church, and the powers of death shall not prevail against it.

- Matthew 16:18

There is a small child. Pale and weak he lies against a white pillow. His lips are blue and his breathing is shallow.

He is your child. You watch him. Every deep breath you take strains at your lungs as you try to breathe for him.

A doctor arrives with a paper in his hands. You are to sign it if your child is going into the operating room for heart surgery. Your hand trembles as you take the pen to sign your name. You are making a commitment. You are committing your child into the hands of this man. It is a statement of your trust in his competence as a heart surgeon.

Part of you wants to cry out loud, "Are you sure you can do it? Will he be all right?" Part of you wants to hold back. Maybe it wouldn't really be necessary. Maybe he would outgrow the heart condition.

But all the time you know you must sign if your child is to have any chance of living. You know this is one time you can't evade a definite commitment. There can be no sitting on the fence.

Peter was faced with the necessity for making a commitment. Jesus asked him, "Who am I?"

Peter could have evaded Jesus. He could have said, "You're Joseph's son, you're our teacher."

But he knew what Jesus was really asking him. He was asking him for a real answer, one that had substance to it. He didn't dodge the question. He didn't laugh it off. He didn't equivocate.

He made a clear, forthright statement of commitment, "You are the Christ, the Son of the living God."

When Jesus heard Peter, he knew that the cause for which he was going to have to give his life was going to succeed despite the mistaken opinions of the masses, the misunderstanding of the intellectuals, the power of the army, the hatred of the entrenched clergy.

For Jesus had penetrated the heart and the mind of Peter. And that was the basis on which he was going to build his kingdom. He needed the commitment of the mind and heart of every man. He wasn't going to have any organization, any army, any political party, any family, any university. All he had was himself and his desire to take every human soul into the presence of God.

This is the commitment every Christian must make beyond whatever other commitments he makes to family, denomination, party, country or cause.

He must be willing to bear the penetrating gaze of Jesus. He must let the consuming love of Jesus destroy the selfishness which is so intimate a part of his being. He must let the terrible truth of Jesus wipe away the falseness behind which he knows he hides.

For Jesus demands commitment to him as the way into the presence of God.

The paper must be signed by you. But even if your hand trembles, he can read the signature and your life is in his hands. Committed to him you become a part of his church, those people who through the ages have kept alive the truth, and the justice, and the mercy and the love of Jesus Christ.

"Forgive me, Lord, for taking so long to make up my mind. My only chance of life is in thy hands. I know this. Give me strength to make that decisive gesture of committing myself to thee. Amen."

MORNING PRAYER

Open your eyes. It's morning.

Like a cat slowly coming to life, I stretch. I breathe deeply. I'm hungry. The thought of cold orange juice frosting the glass, of bacon curling in the frying pan and the aroma of coffee boiling makes me eager to get out of bed.

But first something else in me wants to be satisfied. I have a soul that is glad to be alive. It's a soul that wants to breathe deeply, to be filled with the presence of God. It's a soul that is hungry for the love of God.

"Oh God, who art ever able to satisfy my soul, I thank thee for this morning and this coming day. Let me use it in a way that will be pleasing to thee. In Jesus' name. Amen."

JESUS SAID:
Simon, son of John, do you love me?

- John 21:17

Dark clouds move swiftly across the moon. The wind blows coldly across the fields. There is no sound but the creaking of tree branches hitting the roof.

A woman stands at the window looking out. She shivers. She is lonely. Her spirit is bleak. She has a sense of foreboding. Something frightens her.

But in the distance she sees a car coming down the road. She hears the familiar purr of the motor. It turns in the drive. Her husband slams the door of the house and calls to the woman by the window.

She runs to him. "Do you love me?" she cries.

"You know I love you," he says as he gives her a hearty squeeze.

Warmth replaces her shivers. Contentment takes away the foreboding. Everything looks bright again.

To be loved is what gives meaning to life. To have someone who cares makes it worthwhile to keep on doing things, to keep trying. We need to be loved. All love relationships are not the same-- that of husband is different from that of child, that of parent is different from that of friend, that of lover is different from that of teacher. We do not experience every kind of love relationship. It is not necessary that we do. The important thing is that we know what it is to be loved and that we are capable of loving in return.

Even Jesus needed to be loved. He had to feel that he had inspired love in someone. For he knew that his life, his sacrifice, his ideas were all wrong if they had not made someone love him even as he had loved them.

Why is it so important to feel loved? The reason is that this is how one learns to love someone else. Love is not a part of one's physical structure like a pituitary gland or a pancreas. Love is learned as a result of living together as human beings.

It is impossible to know love without knowing another human being. However, it is possible to know other human beings without knowing love. Where does love come from? It would appear to be a spiritual quality that is born in a person out of a relationship with someone else. It is an intangible quality that might give rise to a variety of definitions depending on the peculiar kind of relationship that has inspired the particular kind of love in a person's life.

But this much is certain. Once love has been experienced, it transcends every other experience in a person's life.

It is the glow from the fire. It is the dancing beam in the sunlight. It is the iridescent shine on the moon. It is the laughing crest on the wave. It is the sparkle in the human eye.

In other words, it is the spiritual quality that makes life a warm, passionate, triumphant gift from a loving God. Love is what makes eternal life desirable for it is a quality that a person never wants to lose. To think that love could die would be the most despairing of all despairs.

Love is what Jesus wanted to inspire in men's hearts. That is why Peter's answer was so vital to Jesus. For once Jesus had inspired love in Peter, then Peter would be able to go on caring for others and that loving spirit could be kept alive in men's souls from generation to generation. Once a person has known the love of God in his life, he knows why he was born and why he wants to exist.

"Dear Lord, as I have known love from other human beings, let me also show love to them. As I have known love from thee, may I also express that love to thee. In Jesus' name. Amen."

MORNING PRAYER

I wonder if *there are more people who get up eagerly in the morning than those who would like to stay a little longer in bed.*

I am among those who get up gladly.

What makes me want to get up?

Curiosity must have something to do with it. I am curious about what the day holds for me. I'm curious about what has happened while I have been asleep. I'm curious about the things I will hear today.

I'm thankful for this curiosity of mine. It has kept life fresh and interesting. It makes people exciting to me. Yes, I'm anxious to get up.

But first, my curiosity has also led me to want to know more about God and in order to know him I pray.

"Oh God, reach into my mind and grasp my thoughts. Lead them toward thee. Stimulate my feelings of adoration, of worship, of praise, for thou art worthy of all these. Take my curiosity and direct it toward understanding thee and thy will for my life. In Jesus' name. Amen."

JESUS SAID:

I am the light of the world; he who follows me will not walk in darkness, but will have the light of life.

- John 8:12

Shadows flicker on the walls across the room. They come and go suddenly. The small boy watches them. His body is tight. It jerks as each new shadow appears. He is frightened. He cannot sleep. He calls, "Mother, may I please have a light?"

"All right," she answers.

He snaps the light above his bed. Everything in the room stands out clearly. No twisting shadows move. He sighs contentedly, turns over and goes to sleep.

He feels more confident when he knows what surrounds him. There is nothing there but what he thought was there, and he knows that will not hurt him.

He has not yet learned to be devious. He does not want to hide. He does not want to be a part of that dark shadowy world where there is no clear distinction between light and darkness, where it is better not to see everything clearly but to disguise it so that it is not what it might seem were the light brighter. Then the gaudiness, the cheapness and the dirt would show.

Now this might be just the kind of world this boy's mother and father prefer--this adult candle-lit club with flickering lights that distort the people as well as hide them from view, a kind of half-world that is an escape from reality.

Here it's not necessary to recognize people or even think about them as people; the empty eyes, the fear-lined forehead, the bored mouth, the angry nostrils, the raucous laugh, the shaking hands are all hid from view. Here no one pays attention to what the other does. There is no censor. It is a popular world, this world of the night.

To many the darkness becomes more attractive than the light. It is a womb to which they scurry to take them away from the world of responsible, caring people.

They don't want to hear Jesus' words. They don't want to see the world clearly. They know what is there and they don't want it. They prefer the darkness. They like a world where no one makes distinctions between right and wrong, between responsible and irresponsible behavior, between duty and pleasure, between morality and immorality.

For Jesus is a light that shows up everything--beauty and blemishes, diamonds and decay, flowers and filth, sickness and health, pomp and poverty. Each person shows up clearly--the way he looks, the way he acts, the way he responds.

Jesus also shows a person the way he should go. He lights up the signs that point the way through life. The mountains are outlined with a fine pencil against a sunny sky. They are there to be climbed.

The prairies and the deserts lay in vast stretches under the hot sun, the torrential rains and the howling winds. They are there to be crossed.

The light shows up all the millions of people scurrying through city streets, idling in cafes, crowding doctors' offices, standing by machines, bank windows and cash registers, driving madly down highways. Everywhere there are people. Jesus says they are there to be loved.

Jesus wants the light to shine into the most furtive corners. He wants things to revealed for what they are. He wants his followers to be honest and to love the light. He wants them to stand in the bright light of day and to have the courage to live in a world where nothing is hidden.

"Forgive me, Lord, the many times I have tried to hide from the light in that dark half-world of the night. Shine brightly on me and give me the strength to see life as it is, to accept it and to live in the full light of thy day. Amen."

MORNING PRAYER

This morning there is a lassitude about me that makes my bed a magnet to keep me here. It is going to take sheer will power to push myself away from it.

Will power is a curious combination of words. They are both nouns. One is not a lesser modifying word. Both are strong words in themselves. Together they make a real force. My will is a power. I can do many things by exerting it, things more important than just getting out of bed, though that is necessary to doing other things. How shall I use it today?

"Dear Lord, I pray thee to help me direct my will into channels for good. Help me to overcome my desire to use it to get my own way either with my family or friends. Make my will power for good. Give me the wisdom to know when to exert it and when not to. In Jesus' name. Amen."

JESUS SAID:
Get behind me, Satan.

- Matthew 16:23

Can you remember what it felt like to be young and daring--to get into a car and to watch that speedometer go up as you pressed on the gas pedal? You grasped the wheel in your hands and you felt the power as you swerved round the curve, then really let go as that straight stretch went right into the horizon.

You were courting danger and you knew it.

Or the time you went nonchalantly into a bar and ordered your first stiff drink?

Or the time you dated that fellow with all the charm and nothing else?

Or the time you cheated on an examination under the very eye of the prof?

You were courting danger and you knew it.

But there was something tantalizing about it. Something in you responded to the daring of it. You wanted to keep company with those suggestive thoughts. You wouldn't let them go. You wouldn't say no to them.

Now Jesus kept company with lots of people, respectable and nonrespectable.

But there was one whose company he did not want. Whenever he came into contact with him, he said, "Get behind me, Satan." He didn't want to look at him. He wanted him thrust out of his sight.

You can be sure Satan was no visible manifestation to Jesus, not Frankenstein's monster or Dr. Jekyll. Satan was the feeling of evil that Jesus senses. This evil crept into his thoughts taunting him, daring him, challenging him. It said, "Try something new. Try something different. Show what you can do. Show what you're really made of. Show them that you are special. There's really nothing wrong with it."

Jesus was a young and caring man. He had great power within himself and he knew it. He was challenged by his place in life. He wanted to succeed.

Remember how much you wanted to succeed, how much you wanted to have your world sit up and take notice of you, how much you desired that boy or that girl. How strong and overpowering those young feelings were! Maybe they still are.

What did you do with them? How did you respond to that tantalizing suggestion of danger, of evil? What is there about evil that draws us to it at the same time we are repulsed by it? Is it the feeling of proving that we can master evil or that we can keep company with it without being tainted by it?

Jesus did not underestimate evil. Jesus did not give himself the strength and the glory with which some men cloak themselves. For Jesus there was only one place for evil - out of his sight and out of his mind. Get away. Depart. Don't hang around me. I don't want your company.

The first time that one says no to evil is usually the hardest--to loose that clutching grip, to turn aside from the dare.

But once evil has gone, God enters in. With God there, everything else seems unimportant.

"Forgive me, Lord, that I expected to be stronger and wiser than you when evil crooked its little finger at me. Like a fool, I went. Like a sinner, I returned. Let me remember to say the words, 'Get behind me, Satan.' Amen."

MORNING PRAYER

That moment before I open my eyes I feel that stirring of excitement in me.

Something is being born--a new day.

A new life holds much promise; so does a new day.

God is giving me something to use, something that is shining with newness.

I am old enough to have learned that if one wants to get the greatest use of a new thing, one must handle it with care.

So...

"Oh God, let me use this day as a gift from thee. Help me to keep it untarnished by cross words; help me to keep its gloss by loving each moment thou hast given me; help me to return it to thee at nightfall unblemished. In Jesus' name. Amen."

JESUS SAID:

Do not marvel that I said to you, 'You must be born anew.'

- John 3:7

Would you really want to be born again?

Would you want to be a young child--looking out on that strange bewildering world of grownups? Would you want to experience that lost, sinking sensation of the first day of school, of seeing the door close on your mother as she leaves you in a strange room with strange people?

Would you want to go through that painful adolescence with its wild ecstasies and unbearable depressions? Would you want to struggle through that mate-searching, job-searching period with its indecision and groping for fulfillment?

Aren't you glad all that is behind you? You have a nice family that you enjoy. You have a job at which you are competent. And you can walk through town without having anyone glare at you.

Is it any wonder that Nicodemus did not exclaim with glee, "Go! Great! Marvelous!," when Jesus told him he had to be born again? Nicodemus was old enough to have made his mark in life. He was a respected man.

He had created a definite personality, so that when people heard the name Nicodemus, a picture of a real man came to their minds. He wasn't anxious to start all over again building a new character when it had taken him all those years to build the one he had.

The only difficulty was that he was not completely satisfied with the character he had. He could feel something tugging at him. A voice was calling to him but he couldn't make out the words. He heard the sound, and he wanted to know what it meant.

Nicodemus had heard Jesus speak and concluded that maybe Jesus could identify this sound for him. He believed Jesus heard that sound, too. So he wanted to talk to Jesus.

Nicodemus was right. Jesus knew what Nicodemus was hearing. It was the voice of the Spirit calling to Nicodemus. But Jesus heard more than just the sound. He heard the words also.

He told Nicodemus that he had been born into a world where he could experience the sensations of touch, sight and smell, where his mind could grow and expand. All this Nicodemus had experienced.

But there was another world into which Nicodemus could be born--a world of the spirit, a world that transcended time and space, a world with no limits, a world as fresh as the morning dew, a world as glowing as the noonday sun, a world that was young and alive, where there was no death because God was there, a God who loved, and in loving made everything alive.

It was a world which Jesus wanted Nicodemus to experience. It meant that Nicodemus needed to let his mind open as a child's, ready to receive what is poured into it. He could not let his mind and spirit be the crotchety mind of an old man. He had to let the Spirit in, to let this God of love mold and reshape his mind. Nicodemus could do this by being willing to be born again.

Many Christians are like Nicodemus. They know there is something more than they have. They have a longing for something. But it takes courage to be born again. To open one's mind to God's invasion means letting down barriers that have been erected to keep a person safe from hurt and harm.

Sometimes the mind has to be softened so that God can reshape it. To believe in God with the innocence of the newborn requires the removal of prejudice, status symbols and prestige props.

"Forgive me, Lord, for letting myself get old when I could be young, for trudging along wearily when I could be flying, for repeating timeworn cliches when I could be thinking of something new, for depending upon past performance to keep me alive. Give me the courage to open up my mind so that it is like a new one. Amen."

MORNING PRAYER

Welcome sun! I see you peeping around the shades. You are teasing me to get up.

Shall I tease you back and just pull the covers over my head so that I cannot see you?

Such childish nonsense with which to begin my day!

Or is it nonsense to love the sun, the rain, the flowers, the trees? Perhaps it is no more nonsense than to love good music, or art, or crafts or books.

In any case...

"Oh God, I thank thee for the world in which I live, for its many desirable things. I love thee for making them. I love thee for letting me live with them. I love thee for thy goodness that shines forth each time I see the morning sun. In Jesus' name. Amen."

JESUS SAID:
Blessed are the meek, for they shall inherit the earth.

- Matthew 5:5

Two men walk across a field.

The one takes long strides, breathing deeply of the crisp morning air. He looks at the dark loam and can already visualize the corn growing straight and tall.

He hears the meadowlark. He stops and watches the throbbing throat of the bird as it sings on a fence post. The man cannot help but feel good as he senses his own healthful vigor, the richness of the soil beneath him and the greeting of the lark. He loves the world within his sight.

Another man walks across the field. He wants to own it. He looks at the soil to figure how many bushels of corn it will yield and imagines how much equipment it would take. With his mind's eye he regards his bank account to figure out what it will look like after he buys this field and produces crops on it for several years. He smiles. That's it. He must own the field.

But what does he really own? He owns the bank account and not the field for he is really not interested in the field. It is the man who loves the field who owns it.

It is the people who love the world who are the inheritors of the world.

There are many people who do not love the world. They want to take possession of whatever world they know so they can change it to fit their ideas.

They are not interested in the natural world with its beauty or its benefits of man. They are only interested in what they can get out of it, so they can do things for their enjoyment, whether it is streaking across the desert in a Jaguar or flying to Alaska for wild game or sailing into the Caribbean for marlin, but always looking for something more to possess.

They are not interested in the social structure of the world with its variety of social units and social relationships. They want to be outside the demands of social institutions - the family, the church, the school, the state. They don't want anyone telling them what to do. They want to make their own plans.

Then there are people like the beatniks who apparently do not even love themselves. They hate their bodies so they do not bother to wash them or to adorn them in any way. They find no beauty to be enhanced.

They do not enjoy their five senses that might find beauty in the out-of-doors--the morning sunrise, the shouts of children playing, the aroma of hamburgers on the open fire or the cold smack of the ocean wave. So they crowd into dark cellars where none of this can penetrate.

You see, the meek people are people who can acknowledge greatness in someone else. They have no trouble acknowledging God--that in his wisdom he created a wonderful world with possibilities for many things. They enjoy the world and its people. They walk through life delighting in the sights and sounds around them. They never believe they have the *right* to own anything except as God grants all men the right to enjoy his world.

They never believe that any person is theirs to own or to control whether it be a child or wife or employee. They can enjoy them, love them, and work with them, but they all belong to the God who made them.

So rather than this making a Christian a sad, bent-over, weary-with-the-world kind of person, it makes him stride through the world, head high, mind alert, heart beating with continuous enjoyment. For, though the world is not his, it doesn't belong to anyone else either. It belongs to God alone and God bestows it on his heirs.

"Thank you, Lord, for making it possible for me to be an heir of thine, for my mind takes delight in thy creation--all of it--even me. Amen."

MORNING PRAYER

The morning is bright with promise.

Promise for what? Promise indicates faith. When I promise my children something, they are are delighted. They are sure they will get it because the word means they can have faith in what I have said. If they can pin me down to a real promise, they know it is as good as done.

God has made promises to man. His promises sound through the Bible like mighty chords playing positive, triumphant notes in a harmony. God has promised me that in every trial, in every tribulation, in every sorrow, in every joy, in every victory, in every task, his love is there to undergird me.

"Oh God, I thank thee for the promise of this day. I have faith in the meaningfulness of my life. Help me to have faith in all that thou hast promised. Help me to keep my promises to others. In Jesus' name. Amen."

JESUS SAID:

Let not your hearts be troubled; believe in God, believe also in me.

- John 14:1

A flag-draped coffin. A hushed church. A heavy heart. A weary spirit. A poignant silence.

Death is here cutting the tie between that person and everyone else. There will be no more talk, no more smiles, no more contact between that person and you. It is such a painful thought that, rather than think about it, you empty your mind of all thought. You stare dully at that altar and the pulpit without really seeing them. You are only vaguely aware of the people sitting near you, silent and saddened by the presence of something no one fully understands.

Slowly the minister comes before the altar. He reads. Habit forces you to listen. Someone else you have not noticed is here. He is asking for your attention. He is saying something to you. Jesus is saying, "Let not your heart be troubled."

How dare he say such words? How hard he must be! Of course your heart is troubled. Why shouldn't it be? Death is terrible, awful, ugly, hateful, and final. Only a callous person could tell you not to be troubled--well, only a callous person or else a person who knows something you don't know. Maybe that is it. Maybe that is why he says that. You are always ready to give Jesus the benefit of any doubts.

What does he seem to know better than you do? He is telling you he knows God better than you do. He is telling you he believes God more than you do.

You have to admit that is true, don't you?

Do you believe in God enough to suffer the torment of a cross and at the same time say that God is love?

Jesus did.

Jesus believed something else, too--at least what he said gives that impression.

Jesus believed that life in God was an eternal thing, that death was not the final word, the grim silencer, the awful robber. Jesus believed this so much he looked upon death as a sleep from which any man could waken, even that criminal who hung on the cross next to him, even as he himself left an empty tomb. Jesus is not evading the fact that death is grim and ugly and devastating and that we must all suffer it, even as he did.

But Jesus is suggesting that we have so much confidence in him and in his words that, even in the agony of death, we can know a hopeful inner peace that comes to the person who has such confidence and faith.

It is a happy thought. Dare you be that happy in the presence of this death that with heartless cruelty strikes every person a lashing blow from which no one seems able to stand up? Do you dare to think that this might not be so final as it appears? Do you tremble a little? Do you feel that it is expecting too much to have our life be more than just a breath that is here today and gone tomorrow? Do you feel foolish thinking this when so many people really do not?

If you dare believe in Jesus, then you dare be just that happy, happy in the thought that death is not final, and that life is a gift from God that is an eternal gift and not just a passing token.

"Dear Lord, help me to believe even when I despair, when I mourn, when I have given up hope. Be my confidence and faith. Amen."

MORNING PRAYER

Somewhere this morning someone is sitting by a quiet lake watching the sun cast its first rays on the water.

Somewhere someone is sitting looking at a craggy mountaintop become gold in the morning sun.

Somewhere someone is riding the mighty ocean where water and sky meet and the morning sun has a watery birth.

But I am in my bed in my house in my community rooted to this little spot I call home. My life is circumscribed by my home but it is also fulfilled in my home.

My imagination can take me to the lake, the forest, the mountains, the ocean. I can breathe the pine-scented air, the salty tang, the misty fog at the same time that I cook and scrub and teach and love the members of my family.

"Oh God, I thank thee for the breadth of the imagination that can take me far and for the depth of the love that keeps me at home. In Jesus' name. Amen."

JESUS SAID:
What is impossible with men is possible with God.

- Luke 18:27

Do you really believe that? Is there a God who can do things man cannot do?

There was a time when men associated God with the thunderclap, the lightning streak, the howling wind, the burning sun, the waving grass. God could make the rain fall, the crops grow and storms cease. God could do all those things that man could not do.

Man has now discovered that he can do many things that he thought were impossible. He can fly beyond the reaches of the sky; he can plummet the ocean's depth. He is on the verge of being able to create life.

Man now believes that he can do the impossible. There is nothing that a god can do that man cannot do. It is true that there are still many things unknown to man--the cure of some diseases, the ability to live in the places beyond the atmosphere and the harnessing of certain natural forces. But these are all things that man is certain he will some day know.

Is this statement of Jesus then wrong? Is it out of date?

Was Jesus talking about a God of magic who could turn mud into gold or cause money to grow on trees or pluck babies from tulips and men from the grave? It is such a God that many men have wanted. It is such a God that would satisfy many men's imaginations.

But that is not the kind of God Jesus knew. Jesus was talking about a God who loved as no one else has ever loved, a God who could enter a man's heart and move him to deeds of compassion and mercy, a God who could cause a man's mind to bow in reverence before the awesomeness of pure love, mercy, compassion, tenderness, justice and integrity.

These are the qualities that are found in God and in him alone and without him they are impossible. Maybe this is why we call these spiritual qualities. They do not come about by a transplant of organs or an injection of liver. They do not come about by flying at a phenomenal speed or lying in air-conditioned comfort. They are not the result of reading the *Encyclopedia Britannica* or learning Sanskrit.

They are the result of coming into the presence of this God who is love, tenderness, mercy and justice. Kneeling at his feet, listening for his voice, singing his praises, thinking his thoughts until they become the center of one's being--this is impossible without the God who is their essence.

It is true that there are irreligious people who have shown mercy and compassion, but to have done so without knowing the God who is their source must be frustrating.

For to be a man without any knowledge of reverence toward God, any knowledge of the consuming love of Jesus, any knowledge of the nature of God, is to be a man whose greatest achievement drains away into nothingness when measured against the joy of the man who walks in the shadow of God.

There are some things that are possible only with God. And only the man who has felt God's presence knows why there are some things that are impossible for men but possible with God.

"Dear Lord, I must acknowledge that there are some things that are impossible for me without thee. Amen."

MORNING PRAYER

At the crack of dawn--crack is such an ugly, harsh word to describe the quietly peaceful coming of dawn -- the light of dawn glows softly. It can't be heard and when it is seen it isn't a little crack of light. It is a light so tremendous that the whole world bathes in it.

"Oh God, who art so generous with us creatures, who hath bestowed on us such abundance, forgive us when we are niggardly and stingy with our possessions, when we keep to ourselves our earthly gifts, talents, our capacity for love. Let us spread about what we have with liberality. As the sun glows in the heavens over all the earth, so may we as Christians glow with unlimited love. In Jesus' name. Amen."

JESUS SAID:
Return to your home, and declare how much God has done for you.

- Luke 8:39

A man claws at his neatly knotted tie. It comes loose. He flings it on the dresser. He pulls off his white shirt, ripping several buttons loose.

He grabs a khaki shirt, changes into khaki pants, runs down the stairs, out the door, takes off from his yard and starts up the mountainside.

He is through with the the dull job, the demanding employer, the irritating salesmen, the self-centered family, the whole frustrating social structure that keeps him from being himself. He is going to leave it all. He is going up to the mountains. He is going to breathe pure air. He is going where there is no one but God. He is going to spend the rest of his life with God. He is going to forget all about people. They ruin everything. They spoil everything that is good. They poison the atmosphere.

There are men who have done just that. They have left the world behind. They have broken their ties with society. They have entered into a life of contemplation, silence and peace.

Having many times in our lives felt the stress and strain of the obligations of a social life, having many times felt the cruel stabs of thoughtless people, having many times been overwhelmed by the crowds pressing in on all sides, perhaps we can sympathize with such desires.

But Jesus does not tolerate such tendencies. When Jesus said, "Return . . .," he had just spent the night with a man whose reason he had restored. This man whose madness had driven him from society wanted to stay with Jesus. He wanted to be with the man who had helped him to find himself. He had talked with Jesus all night and he wanted to stay with him. Surely this was understandable. He didn't want to return to the world where men would remember his madness, where men would no doubt taunt him. He felt the need of Jesus. He needed the sustaining strength of another person.

But Jesus told him he must go back; not only must he go back but he must talk to people, must tell them what God meant to him.

This was not an easy task Jesus gave this man. It seemed to be expecting a great deal.

This is probably just why it was such a tremendous cure. Because Jesus expected hard things of this man, it made him realize that he must actually be capable of doing this or Jesus could not ask it of him. This was a real restoration of confidence.

For, to Jesus, God is not a means of escaping from the world. God is means for living in the world.

Each one of us is a part of the crowd, belongs in the social structure, serves a purpose and is also served by this society. There is no shaking off our humanity. There is no escaping it. We cannot flee from it for then we would no longer be human.

And God loves this strange, bewildering, maddening humanity.

Sometimes this is hard to remember. It is not only I whom God loves. It's all those other people, too. God does not single out certain people to lure them away from humanity. His love encompasses us all. A person responds to God's love by coming to grips with humanity - by serving humanity, by talking with humanity, by living with humanity.

Jesus sent this man home to do just that.

Did he ask more of this man than he asks of me?

"Dear Lord, help me to remember that I am frequently just as irritating and provoking as many other people. If you are going to love me who am this way, so will you love those others who are also this way. Amen."

MORNING PRAYER

It is so pleasant to wake in the morning in my own house with my own family nearby. I know there is food for breakfast, I have clothes to slip into, and I have a community of stores and public services that are open for me.

What would it be like to be one of the many who wake knowing there is no food for breakfast, who wake in a dingy cellar or prison, or mud hut, who wake cold and miserable, who wake in a hospital bed where waves of pain assault them? I cringe at the thought, yet I must not.

As a Christian, as a member of the human race, compassion must enter my thoughts and cause me to pray . . .

"Oh Father in heaven, I pray thee for all my fellow-men who are in suffering and need. Send thy balm to heal their sick bodies and souls. Send thy abundance to meet their needs and make me realize that thy love for them and thy comfort for them can come from me and others like me who have while they have not and who know thy love while others do not. In Jesus' name. Amen."

JESUS SAID:
For the Son of man came to seek and save the lost

- Luke 19:10

All he sees around him is a forest of legs--the small child is lost in the crowd. No familiar voice calls his name. No hand is reaching for him. He is alone to stumble round and round. He is mute with terror.

That never happens to you any more, does it? You know your way around. You can see and read the street signs. You are an expert with maps. You know how to ask your way if you are in a strange place. You know where you are going and how to get there.

The word "lost" does not apply to you any more.

In a way it is a pity for, since you are not lost, Jesus need not seek you. He seems to be looking for lost people.

He is looking for people who don't know all the answers.

He is looking for people who need help to find their way.

He is looking for people whose feeling of being lost has made them quiet with despair for they are --

Lost, even though they know their way confidently in the world of the arts--music, drama, painting and sculpture.

Lost, even though they have opened their minds to the writings of the philosophers - Socrates, Kant, Buber.

Lost even though they walk with poise in the company of lawyers, politicians, professors, businessmen and the clergy.

Lost, even though their families live in one of the better parts of town and their social calendars are full.

They know they are lost because they feel so alone when they think about it. They feel that much of what they do has no meaning. They wonder why they keep going at all. They are like the little child who wanders round and round helplessly because he doesn't know the way home.

And they, like him, know they are lost. In their quiet terror maybe they will hear the Shepherd's voice, maybe they will yearn for his hand, maybe they will recognize him when he comes.

For Jesus is looking for them. Is there anyone else who is?

Has anyone else expressed concern for the lost? Does anyone else claim to be able to help the lost?

Jesus said many things about himself, but he never said he was lost. He knew God and he knew the way to him. His relationship with God was such that God was with him everywhere. God made clear to him the interpretation of the events of his life so that it was never meaningless to him even when he had to be willing to give his life in what to most men would have seemed a meaningless gesture. What under the sun could be accomplished by dying? But he gave meaning even to dying.

In this maze of events that we call our life, Jesus is ready to interpret for us a direction and a focus for them. But we must be willing to acknowledge that he knows the way, and that he has interpreted the mind of God in a much clearer way than we ever can.

"Forgive me, Lord, for not admitting that many times I feel lost. The many happenings of my life crowd around me sometimes, making me feel as if I am going to choke for lack of air. I need thy voice to give meaning to what I do and to set my steps on a path that goes somewhere. Amen."

MORNING PRAYER

I have just opened my eyes.

I don't even know what day it is but there will be something to do. There always is. Every single day makes its demands.

Sometimes I wish I could wake up with not a thing to do. But really, when I think about it I realize it would be dreadful. Imagine-- just nothingness. What if there were just nothingness!

The thought makes me shudder, and it makes me pray.

"Oh Lord, I thank thee for all thou hast created out of nothingness. I thank thee most of all for the people thou hast created--my family, my friends, the great men and women of the past, all those who serve humanity today. May I do my share. In Jesus name. Amen.

JESUS SAID:

Is it lawful on the sabbath to do good or to do harm, to save life or destroy it?

- Luke 6:9

Only someone from the North who has lived through a long, dismal winter can truly fall in love, fall in love with spring, I mean. Those warm breezes from the South, the ground getting spongy underfoot, the smell of green things sprouting, and a sun whose warmth is no longer an illusion, contain all the promise of a beautiful love affair.

Don't you remember as a child sitting in a schoolroom on that first spring day staring out the window watching the white clouds bouncing on that blue ceiling, wishing, wishing you could be outside? Suddenly you hated the stuffy smell of chalk dust, the drone of your teacher's voice, the sight of the worn-out textbook on your desk, the sounds of the pens scratching on paper. You wanted to get out, to run free across the meadows.

You knew school was important, lessons were important, routine was necessary. But just this once you'd like to forget it all, to revel in freedom from restraint, freedom from the law.

Jesus is hardly talking about playing hooky from school. Ah, but maybe he is. Maybe one day it would be more important for a child to do something other than go to school. It is true that ordinarily he should go to school, but to be so hidebound by the law that the child could never miss school might be wrong. To make perfect attendance the highest good might be exactly what the Pharisees would advocate, and Jesus tangled with them on the occasion that inspired these words as well as on many others.

The law, customs, and rules have developed as instruments for the good of society--usually. People live in a society governed by law, and it is good that they respect the law. A child grows up in a family where there are certain customs, and it is good for him to observe them. A church makes rules by which it is governed, and its adherents should be loyal to them.

Laws, customs and rules are passed from generation to generation. Yet each generation is different so that the laws, the customs and the rules are always subject to reinterpretation to meet the needs of the new generation. Some new laws must be made and some old ones discarded.

Now there are people who learn to love the laws, the customs and the rules more than they love the people for whom they are made. They become rigid.

There comes a time when the law must be defied. There come times when the rule needs to be disobeyed. There come times when the custom must be broken. For God's spirit is a great, free, soaring spirit that sometimes sweeps a man beyond the ordinary scope of the law to taste and to see and to feel a freedom that is not bound by law. And sometimes a Christian has to act within that freedom.

However, a Christian never breaks the law for personal gain or for the pure joy of rebelling. A Christian breaks the law only when a higher good demands it. And the Christian looks at the law always as the servant of mankind, never as its god.

As a result for the Christian, the law never stands as a grim fortress that protects him from evil but keeps him penned in from the sun as well. Instead, the law is a white fence showing him the bounds of lawful behavior but having in it a gate that can be easily unlatched when necessary.

"Forgive me, Lord, the times when I, like the Pharisee, could not see beyond the law to the great mercy of God, when I clung to the law even when it meant hurting a creature of thine. Yet, let me never defy the law for selfish purposes of my own, for the law, also, is revealed to men so that they might better live within the framework of a good society. Amen."

MORNING PRAYER

Dare I open my eyes this morning?
Dare I face a day in this world that is trembling with revolution?
Sometimes it seems that the foundations of institutions that were so secure are shaking. There is no solid ground anywhere.

But I'm not the first to feel this way. Long, long ago the psalmist said, "Therefore we will not fear though the earth should change, though the mountains shake in the heart of the sea."
He could not have written that had he not first known the fear.

"Oh God, each generation has had reasons to be fearful, but in each generation there have also been men of faith. They knew that thou wast there with them in their moral struggles with the power of evil. Thou art also here now. For this I do praise and adore thee. In Jesus' name. Amen."

JESUS SAID:
Do not be afraid; henceforth you will be catching men.

- Luke 5:10

Are you a user of the words, "I can't?"

"I can't be an officer. I can't teach. I can't speak. I can't play tennis. I can't swim."

Maybe you have even said, "I can't be a good husband or wife. I can't be a good mother or father. I don't have what it takes."

Now it is admirable to know and to admit one's limitations for music or football or for acting or for hiking.

But think about the times you say, "I'm sorry. I can't."

Wouldn't it be truer for you to say at those times, "I'm sorry. I won't"?

It is so much easier to shift the blame for one's lack of responsibility to nature or to stupidity or to humility or even to one's Creator than to one's unwillingness to be concerned.

You know, often one's knowledge of oneself is limited by one's efforts. Some people never try. They are afraid of failing or of looking foolish or being embarrassed. They expect little of themselves and they get little.

If they can't get something the first time they try it, they say they can't. They never feel the challenge of the difficult or the exultation that comes with the acceptance of a task that is going to be demanding and that is going to take all one's best effort.

Faith requires of a man that he do something even if he is afraid that he might fail.

Jesus had a big job for the fishermen. He wanted them to persuade people to a new way of life, to disturb the old grooves in their brains, to reroute their familiar thought impulses. Is there anything harder?

Think about yourself. Don't you cling to your own ideas stubbornly? Are you eager to have someone change your mind?

Yet this is what the disciples were called upon to do--to change men's minds, to make them over, to give them something new to think about and to show them a new God (not really a new God but a new understanding of him).

No wonder they were afraid. And so far they just had the merest glimmer of what Jesus was going to demand of them. No wonder Jesus had to say, "Do not be afraid!"

But they did follow him. They did undertake the big task even though they found out that it was much harder than they expected, that there was no sudden glory in it, and that they had to walk a slippery and dangerous path.

Yet though they often trembled and almost gave up, Jesus' words had made such an impression on them that when everything seemed hopeless, they were able to show courage and to make their quaking legs stand firm.

You are a Christian today because they were able to heed Jesus' words, "Do not be afraid."

And maybe the next time you start to say "I can't," you may bring to your mind the picture of those few fishermen whose lives were completely changed because rather than say "I can't " to Jesus they followed after him.

"Forgive me, Lord, for saying 'I can't' so often. Let me feel instead the thrill of trying something hard. When I look at myself, let me see a person who isn't afraid to try, who isn't afraid of exposure. Let me join the company of the disciples who came to know you and your purposes because they were willing to try. Amen."

MORNING PRAYER

In a moment, as soon as I pull the curtains, I shall be bathed in light.

This life is so amazing I can see far across the river to the hills on the other side. I can see the houses of my neighbors that were just a short time ago shrouded in darkness.

In spring I look out on a soft green world that is cool and moist.

In summer I see the darker greens that often become brown and hazy in the heat.

In autumn I see hillsides of light yellows, lovely reds and muted browns.

In winter I see black, bare branches etched against gray skies.

"Oh God, let my senses thrill to thy creativity that is new every morning. Even though I grow old, my spirit can be renewed each morning by the ageless touch of thy hands. In Jesus' name. Amen."

JESUS SAID:
Heaven and earth will pass away, but my words will not pass away.

- Mark 13:31

Words are sounds that hover in the air for an instant and then are gone. A person coming into the room where the words were spoken would have no evidence that they had ever been uttered.

Think of the enduring quality of steel or stone or marble. It is big and heavy to move. It is hard and resistant to change. It sits impervious to wind and rain and snow, to birds and snakes and butterflies.

But a word strikes the air without shape or form or color and like a breath it is gone.

Yet Jesus said that, though everything else passed from existence, his words would remain.

Such a confident statement to make! He was not even writing his words on paper. No reporter was sitting there to take his words in shorthand. His words were just passing through the brain cells of a few very vulnerable human beings like you and me. How many words do you remember of all those you hear?

If you think about it, you really do remember quite a few. Many of them you pass on to your family, your associates, your friends. And they, in turn, pass them on. But once out of your mouth, they usually become someone else's words. And you don't hear your words quoted back to you as you once said them. Your words are lost forever.

But Jesus' words have endured. His words with his trademark on them have been preserved. The Temple was smashed, Jerusalem was destroyed, even Rome was ravaged. Only broken shards buried under sand remain from that period of history.

But we hear Jesus' words today. We hear them often, from the time we are small children until the last moment in the cemetery. More people hear them today than when Jesus formed those sounds that made words.

In fact, many words have come down to us through the ages from many people, long after everything else about them has disappeared—their bodies, their homes, their cities.

Words are the means of conveying thought. And isn't thinking man's most important function? Jesus says that it is the product of his thought that he is passing on to men. The way he passes it on is through their thought processes, for this is the only way words can be passed - from one thinking, understanding man to another.

Actually no power in the world is more powerful than man's thought. It is this that makes it possible for man to fly to the moon and to live under the sea. This is the power that Jesus wants in each man--his thinking power. The way to enter a man's thought is by words, words that a man remembers, that make him think and act in a certain way.

In the swift-moving, material-oriented world, the role of the teacher, the preacher and the librarian--the custodians of words--sometimes appears insignificant. But this is good. Maybe their lack of splash and publicity, their very colorlessness, their reserved decorum, are what keep them safe, safe to pass on this greatest power in the world, this power of human thought conveyed in words.

Their business goes on unobtrusively in each generation without the glamor of other roles. But the true teacher, the true preacher, the true librarian is so concerned with human thought, he loses himself in the wonder of the words he is passing on.

"Make me understand and appreciate, Lord, the words I have learned that are thine. Help me to understand what a power they can be in my life. Help me to live by them and help me to pass them on so that I, too, may help preserve thy words in time. Amen."

INTRODUCTION
On Being and Evening Prayer

These short meditations cover a wide range of human characteristics Ruth saw in herself and others. She explores our identities at a deeper level than those associated with our social roles, even though these characteristics develop in our social relationships. They are traits of personality and character, shaped by the Christian faith which she describes with ironic humor that often turns our thoughts about them in a surprising direction. Being casual is not always appropriate; being a hater is sometimes most appropriate--to cite two examples.

These writings are not the kind we keep because they have information we may need in the future. They are glimpses of ourselves that provide insight. Consider them as the beginnings of conversations with her and respond to them from your own experience and insight, whether or not you agree. Someone tells you a story or makes a statement that reminds you of a similar experience so you respond by sharing your story or saying. That is the way to read these writings. If you are inclined, write down a conversation. This is one form of meditation, an offspring of one traditionally called *lectio divina*, divine reading, a way of reading the Bible meditatively.

ON BEING A CHILD

I might as well skip this page. This isn't for me. I'm no child. Every aching bone and gray hair tells me I am no child.

But wait. Do you remember?

Do you remember the feel of cool green grass between your toes as you ran barefoot across the lawn?

Do you remember waiting for the sound of the ice-cream vendor as he made his rounds on a hot summer day? Do you remember the luscious taste of that red, sweetened ice?

Do you remember exploring among rocky ledges, or noisy railroad yards, or huge bridge girders or endless sandy beaches?

Do you remember the terror of being lost - in a crowded department store filled with unrecognizable legs, or at a county fair with the creaking Ferris wheel and the gaudy prizes, or in a wood filled with crackling branches and hooting animals?

Do you remember the flow that came from the master of something new - the triumph of learning to tie your own shoes, of balancing a two-wheel bike for the first time or seeing a printed page and being able to read it?

Do you remember the agony of guilt, the time you ripped your new clothes climbing the tree you weren't supposed to climb before Sunday school? The time you told your mother you had not eaten the candy when you knew you had? The time you shouted at your parents "I hate you!" when you were not permitted to do what you wanted to do?

Do you remember the night when you awakened from a frightful dream to call out, "Mother!" She came. Do you remember the bliss of her voice, the soothing coolness of her hands?

You do remember, don't you?

Think about it. What is so different now?

You still feel--maybe not in your bare feet, but in your soft slippers.

You still taste--maybe not Popsicles, but a lobster dripping in butter.

You still explore--maybe not a rocky ledge, but from an armchair with a good book.

You still know the terror of being lost--in a world of pain, or insecurity or death.

You still can glow--when you are praised by your boss, or your wife, or your congregation or your children for something you have done.

You still can feel guilty--for those many things you have failed to do, for the wasted moments, for the self-seeking that drives you.

You still can turn in your fright to call out, "O God!"

You can never escape being a child. You never really become a master. You are a child by nature. You cannot be anything else.

You cannot be a god. You have no say about your destiny.

It is in the hands of him who made you.

Therefore it seems it would be wise to enjoy being a child--to enjoy feeling, tasting, learning. It would be wise to know that when the terror of being lost, being guilty and being frightened tends to overwhelm you, you know where to turn.

For you are a child of God forever.

If you cannot say this with a feeling of gratitude, joy and happiness, you will be miserable for you cannot escape your nature.

The child who knows he is a child, who knows that he needs to learn, who eagerly soaks up the knowledge that is offered to him is the child whose stature lengthens, whose eyes take on wisdom, and whose heart opens with compassion to the world around him.

He is the child who instinctively cries, "O God," when his heart trembles within him.

It is as Jesus said, "Except ye become as a little child . . ."

EVENING PRAYER

Sleep is a wonderful thing--to see a child lying completely relaxed, its little body warm and soft. It is delightful to feel the lassitude that comes just as I am about to fall asleep, as if the body and brain are giving in for a little while, no more demanding energy to be spent.

It must have been the most wonderful thing that could happen to her when Jesus told the mother, "Your daughter is not dead. She only sleeps."

For sleep is a healthy, blessed thing.

"Oh God, I thank thee for sleep that comes to bring my body rest, that gives it a chance to create more energy for the day ahead. Grant sleep to all who are tired from work, or pain or sorrow. In Jesus' name. Amen."

ON BEING A PARENT

"We are going to have a baby," a wife tells her husband. The response may be joy and elation or it may be consternation depending on the circumstances. But there is a response!

For a baby is a thing to be reckoned with. Once a baby arrives, the carefree days are gone. That little dimpled, soft-skinned baby twines its fingers around yours, never really to let go. Physically that baby may some day go to Lapland or New Zealand, but emotionally the tug of that small finger is always there, pulling at your thoughts, at your memories, at your prayers.

I suppose most people want to become parents want to have the chance to mold the life of a human being want to extend themselves into another generation.

But once they have become parents, I'm sure no parent would challenge the statement that, "There is no harder job in the world than to be a good parent."

What constitutes a good parent?

A good parent protects his child but how far? Shall the child be isolated from other children to keep him free from germs and bodily injury? Shall he be taken to school to keep him from being run over? Shall he be taken to the doctor for every little cold? Shall he be kept from dating a Roman Catholic to prevent the possibility of such a marriage? How many times does a parent have to decide where the line between proper care and overprotection lies? Each time the child ventures out, this decision has to be faced.

A good parent gives his child good things--food, clothing, books, toys, recreation--but how much? Where is the line between adequate loving consideration and overindulgence? Each time the child asks for something (which is frequently!) this decision has to be faced.

A good parent gives his child an education, but what kind? Shall he make him take piano lessons? Shall he help him write his themes or do his arithmetic? Shall he insist he have a liberal arts education if he wants to be a mechanic? Shall he make him go to Harvard or Wittenberg or Gustavus if he wants to go to Texas? To what extent should the wider perspective from which the parent views life be forced upon the child who cannot see the things the parent sees? How much can the parent see for him?

A good parent gives a child emotional security, but in what way? He has to punish him for wrongdoing at the same time that he has to forgive him for wrongdoing. He has to teach him to be kind at the same time he has to teach him to be tough. He has to teach him principles at the same time he has to teach him to be tolerant. He has to teach him modesty without teaching him shame. He has to teach him to be independent at the same time he has to teach him to have gratitude to others.

A good parent gives his child religious concepts, but when? Shall he teach him the Ten Commandments, the Lord's Prayer, the Apostles' Creed, the Bible stories? Of course. But when? Shall he teach him the meaning of myth, of historical criticism, of the ecumenical church? Of course. But when? Can a parent really teach a child to pray, to worship, to adore, to love God? Or can he only give a good example?

To be a truly good parent seems to be an impossible task. And it would be an intolerable burden were it not for the quality of love that enters into his parent-child relationship. Love makes it possible for the parent to forgive, for the child to understand. Love makes it possible to view the erratic behavior of the adolescent with humor and with forbearance. Love makes it possible to laugh over foolish mistakes and to cry over serious ones. Love makes it possible to talk to each other. When a parent and child can talk to each other, they can often smooth the difficulties as each sees the other's point of view. A hug, a kiss, a smile can work wonders in those electric moments that come in every family.

To some Christians, being a Christian is a burden because they are always trying to live up to Christ instead of living in Christ, in his forgiveness, in his grace.

To some parents, being a parent is a burden because they are always trying to live their children's lives instead of trying to live for their children's lives. Instead of taking them as they are, they take them as they want them to be. But God is the Creator of each child.

His ways and plans are infinitely wiser than the parents'.

A parent cannot escape the decisions that have to be made each day. That is why it is important each day for each parent to pray for wisdom, for understanding and for love.

But most of all for love. A parent should love his child, even as God loves him.

EVENING PRAYER

Sometimes I feel that night is like a gracious mother tucking me into the soft darkness, taking away my cares and troubles. Sometimes I feel that night is like a furtive thief filling me with fears and anxieties about what I have done and what the future holds.

Sometimes I am too tired to feel at all.

But in whatever state I am, I pray.

"Oh Lord come to me in the darkness. Help me to remember thy unceasing care and love for all mankind. In Jesus' name. Amen."

ON BEING A READER

Reading is really a way of life. It has an existence of its own.

When I read, I talk, I walk, I eat, I climb mountains, I bathe in warm waters, I protest against sordidness, I weep at cruelty, I laugh at the ridiculous, I worship the holy.

I meet the psychologist, the philosopher, the artist, the musician, the sportsman, the preacher, the Republican, the Democrat, the Communist, the housewife, the lawyer.

I wander through small towns, great cities, strange countries aboard trains, planes, ships and all kinds of animal transportation.

I become acquainted with people, people who are real and people who are imagined. But they are people who I learn to know and to love. Their lives touch mine.

I feel pain and joy. I feel birth and death. I feel laughter bubbling and tears rising.

A book made of paper and ink can be all these things. Words, all contrived from 26 letters, can accomplish this.

To teach a child to read is to give him a world.

This is a world that everyone reading this book can have. Libraries are waiting for readers. A librarian's greatest joy is seeing that a book is read. A library's existence depends on this.

But there are so many books, I could not even begin to touch them all.

Not all books are good.

I used to feel that once I started a book, I was obliged to finish it. I don't feel that way any more. The time I have to spend reading is too precious. If the book does not answer a need or introduce me to something new or demand my attention, I often do not finish it for I can always find one that does do these things.

I read just for fun, too. I have laughed more heartily at books of humor than I have ever laughed at a comedian. I can get intrigued by a mystery that unravels much too slowly for my curiosity. I can also read cookbooks and find myself with drooling taste buds at midnight, at least eight hours away from the nearest meal.

I remember well the day I discovered that books were really a new world. I was six years old, and my father took me to the public library to get a card. The librarian suggested that *The Sunbonnet Babies* would be about my reading level. I took two of them home with me, and by supper I had finished both and wanted to return to the library for more. From then on the library became my second home.

Another important reading remembrance is a day when I was 17. It was in the summer. I was bored. I had read my own books many times. I went into my father's study thinking that by some remote chance I might find among the Hebrew and Greek grammars, the Bible commentaries, and the works of Luther a book I could read.

I picked up a little book, *Why I Am A Christian*. I started to read and I was fascinated. Questions I had often thought but never expressed were discussed. I have since found new insight into being a Christian, but that book helped set me on my way.

So another world opened up for me--one that has never ceased to be interesting--the world of religious writing. I exhaust one author only to find there is another with new and intriguing insight. I go back to reading the Bible with new appreciation.

The Bible--now there is a book. As a child, I read it for its stories. As a teenager, I read it for its poetry and its advice. As an older person, I read it because I need it. I need it to keep my mind aware of ultimate things when immediate things are so pressing. I need it to remind me that I have a loving Father at a time I no longer consider myself a child. I need it because it helps me to know God who I need very much.

Books--I love them.

EVENING PRAYER

I'm tired but I'm not sleepy.

Maybe thinking about quiet things will make me sleepy --a soft snowflake floating soundlessly through a wintry sky; a still lake under a full moon, its glassy surface unmarred by even a ripple; a high-vaulted empty church with its heavy doors shut to the muffled noise outside; an unspoken prayer winging its way from my mind to the eternal mind of God.

"Oh God, be near me tonight. I need thy presence to refresh my weary mind. I need thy forgiveness for the guilt I feel. I pray thee to be with my family. In Jesus' name. Amen."

ON BEING CONSERVATIVE

I am a conservative--cautious, careful, prudent, a lover of history, of family, of nationality, of race.

I think I was born that way. As a child, if the lake was declared safe for ice-skating one day, I waited at least three more days of sub-zero weather to be *sure* it was safe.

If it was a good idea to say, "Now I lay me down to sleep," once before going to sleep, I said it three times each night to be *sure* the Lord would hear me.

If it took ten minutes to walk to school, I always left at least one-half hour earlier to be *sure* I got there on time.

I never took a dare in my life--until I got married. Even though marriage was an institution which conservative people had endorsed for many centuries, I thought it might be too radical an adjustment for me, although I was marrying a man of the same national background, same denomination and same college class!

Since I had always been such a careful, cautious, conservative character, I had had my own way in life, even with my friends. My arguments were always reasonable. I was sure I could manage the same way with a husband.

But I was in for a surprise. He was really unmanageable. Our first argument came when we were going to cut the wedding cake. He had his own idea about how that should be done. My reasonable suggestions did not seem at all reasonable to him.

I can't remember how it turned out, but he must have won because the cake got cut, and I'm sure he didn't give in.

On our honeymoon we were riding along blissfully in the car through the new spring green of the New Hampshire mountains. Somehow we got on the subject of labor and capital (must have been *his* idea!). We got to arguing so vehemently, he had to stop the car by a grove of pine trees because it wasn't safe to drive. We paced back and forth shouting our points of view at each other. My reasonable arguments didn't impress him in the least.

We finally changed the subject and drove off.

This tug-of-war had some violent outbursts in our early married life--my whole way of life was threatened. He never got ready early for anything except church, and he was highly amused to have me sitting with my coat on when he hadn't even shaved. "Imagine wasting all that time doing nothing," he'd say.

Guess who are now the last ones to arrive at almost everything! But it is really amazing how much I can get done in that time I used to spend waiting for the program to begin or the other guests to arrive.

Do you remember when the new hymnal came out? It meant a rather drastic change in our church. I thought the old hymnal was fine. I loved the old service. I wanted nothing to do with this hymnal. I practically hit the ceiling (and our church has a high one) when I heard the pastor chant part of the service for the first time. Naturally, my husband liked it.

Then he began his usual patient indoctrination with his reluctant wife and I became an appreciative participant. Worship became meaningful and my heritage was enriched.

Any music written after Bach was not music to me. My husband, of course, thought jazz was great--in addition to Bach, naturally. Recently we got a stereo record of the liturgy done to a jazz tempo. Had this occurred a few years ago, I would have thought it musically obscene. But because of my conditioning over the years, I found myself putting that record on again and again. When they sang the Nicene Creed, I put it on at full power until it rang across the valley and hit the hills on the other side and my house shook with the glory of it.

I think often how dull my life would be without a husband who is always excited by new thoughts, new ways of doing things, new people. He is never satisfied to do anything the same old way. He is always sure there is a better way. This means, of course, that he is never content as I often am, just the way things are. He is always stretching and always reaching.

And I have thought how much more strength it takes to be growing both downwards and upwards than it takes to keep one's roots always in the same place. Yet, those of us who are conservative seem to feel that we are the ones who are wise. We are not always wise, sad to say, but we are usually smug.

My reason for writing this is that I have observed in the church much contentment with the conservative point of view. It is usually a real battle to get a congregation to accept anything new whether it is in the form of a new hymn, or a new kind of architecture or a new program. By the time the church moves, it is usually lagging way behind every other organization.

Yet the church should be a tree that towers above all the rest. But its roots are so firmly entrenched in the grounds of the past that instead of growing upward it spreads its roots all over the place so that it actually chokes out some of the new shoots that are trying to send forth roots.

The sad thing is that Jesus planted a seed that was meant to grow and stretch and fling great branches toward the heavens. For Jesus was the greatest advocate of change who has ever lived. How he hated the whited sepulchers dedicated to the past! He demanded a completely new way of life.

I know how hard it is to change. It causes real emotional upheaval for me to do it. But I have also discovered it is the only way to grow and to become enriched.

And the church needs to grow. It needs to be challenged in this age of great problems. It needs to be threatened, for that is often the only way it will move at all. To be looking for something new is not deserting the past, it is fulfilling the past--just as Jesus did. The only way to make our forefathers' work worthwhile is to be adding to it.

The church needs to look at its Master who was a new spirit, a new breath of life in a fading, dying, decadent society. The roots are there, but the church needs to send its strength upward and outward into every segment of life through every Christian who claims Christ as his Savior.

EVENING PRAYER

Sometimes time frightens me. It is so relentless. There is no way to stop it. It is like a mad, rushing river that tumbles over everything in its path.

Another day has been carried by its current into the sea of infinity. I have little to show for it except that the aging process has gone on in me, and I am very tired.

But not too tired to pray.

"Oh God, who art greater than time, who are not bound by its steady tread, who hast no beginning and no end, grant me the peace that comes from knowing that I, too, might share the timelessness if I put myself in the shadow of thy love and care. In Jesus' name. Amen."

ON BEING A DREAMER

I remember as a child waking in terror, my heart beating wildly, my legs incapable of movement as a creature with evil intent sprang at me.

It was only a dream.

I remember sitting at my desk in school staring at the clouds out the window, clouds that took me to a horse ranch, or on an ocean voyage or to the great desert where I rode on a camel and ate fresh dates.

It was only a dream.

I remember sitting at a ball game, my eyes glued to a particular boy while I went walking with him along the beach at the seashore, or through the meadows in the moonlight or clasping his hand as we gaily tried the night life of the big city.

It was only a dream.

Asleep or awake, I dream.

I have no control over the dreams I have when I sleep. But my waking dreams--that is another story.

It is so easy, so pleasant to dream. I remember riding with my parents on a trip, the back seat all to myself while I spun dream after dream, dreams filled with lovely people, exciting moments and amazing triumphs.

I was always considered a good child because I was so quiet in church, at meetings and in adult groups. Actually, I was far away having a most exciting time. I was giving a political speech, or singing in grand opera (you should hear me sing!) or performing a rare operation to save someone's life.

I was about five years old when I discovered that human beings could dream while they were awake. I had been put to bed for a nap but I couldn't go to sleep. So I just lay there. And just like that, very suddenly, I discovered I could make up things in my mind. What fun!

It was like finding a friend, someone with whom to spend those many moments that a child has when he is young with nothing to do.

My dream world reached its peak in my teens. A teen-ager has a hard time finding himself. He doesn't know what is proper, what will make him appear the most adult. In dreams it is so easy. I took the easy way out. I became a dreamer.

Then, when I was a college freshman, a professor told me in no uncertain terms that I had chosen a dangerous avocation.

"Dreams have their limit. You are not living in a dream world. This world is real. It's tough, and you have to face it. Now get out on that campus and do something. Join every club that will have you. Find out what it is like to live in a world of human beings, not one of dream creatures. Find out what boys are really like, not what you would like them to be."

His remarks shook me. No one had ever spoken that bluntly to me before.

But I took his advice and entered upon the happiest years of my life. I discovered people. Oh, I was hurt many times. But I also found out what love was, the kind of love that human beings have for one another, the warm, forgiving, loyal, tender love. Maybe I was in a good place to become aware of people because there were so many wonderful ones around.

That professor was wrong about one thing though. The boys I met were much more interesting than the ones I dreamed about.

The challenge to keep alive these human relationships, to be interesting enough for people to want my company, to find ways of participating in group activity made me come alive, made me feel intensely, made me belong to the human race, not the Ruth race.

Worship became more meaningful to me when I did it with other people. God became less dream-like and more real. Jesus was not so much the person with whom to stroll in the garden as the suffering humane God who made me aware of mankind's wounds that needed healing.

To use dreams to escape from reality is sheer deviltry.

To use dreams to meet reality to find solutions to problems, to use imagination to figure out new ways to help mankind, to use the mind to create new situations, this is a gift from God.

This kind of dream plunges a person into the center of life.

I hope we meet there.

EVENING PRAYER

Really I think I have had a good day. But I must confess I am exhausted. I can feel the weary beat of my heart as it thumps patiently within me.

What a welcome spot is my bed with its soft mattress, its warm covers! I look forward to the dropping of sleep over me as if I were a dry and thirsty flower cupping the rain within its petals.

As a child I pushed open heavy lids to resist sleep. Now that I am grown, I close my lids while I am still awake.

As a child I prayed. Now that I am grown I still pray.

"Dear God, as I lie on my bed I thank thee for the day now past. If I fail to recognize each day as a gift from thee, forgive me. As I lie in safety, I pray for those who have no pillows for their heads, whose bed is hard and unyielding. I pray for those who might have pillows for their heads and silk sheets for their bodies but who do not know the comfort of thy Presence. In Jesus' name. Amen."

ON BEING HONEST

Purple leaves hung silent from the trees.
The lake was still.
A fish jumped.
The clear glassy water broke into pieces.
A small boy stood on the shore.   He watched the pieces break.
Then he watched them come together again, as still and smooth as if the surface had never been broken.

The purple leaves were getting darker.
The little boy shivered as he looked at the black water.
But he couldn't seem to move.
A voice was calling from a distance.
He turned from the water to go along the path through the dark, whispering trees.
He looked frightened.

Then a single star came out in the not-quite-black sky.
Suddenly he picked up his feet and ran toward the voice.
"Where have you been?" the voice asked anxiously.
"By the lake," he answered breathlessly. "I was afraid. But then I saw God's eye looking at me from the sky. And I ran home."

Sweet, isn't it? But is it honest?
Leaves aren't purple. They are green. They only look purple in the sunset.
Water doesn't break into pieces. It just redistributes itself.
Trees don't whisper. They make a noise as they move.
A star is not God's eye. It is a planet millions of miles away, cold and forbidding.

To create an effect, I have used images that I have made with words. They are not actually accurate. People who write do this with words. People who paint do this with colors. People who act do it with motions and inflections.

Really, each one of us does it. We each create an image of ourselves that we want people to see. As children, we are taught very early to *behave*, to create a good image of ourselves for other people.

The image we create for our parents is different from the one we want to create for our friends. The image we create for our teachers is different from the one we create for our brothers and sisters. We create new images as new demands are made upon us.

We are conditioned to do this so much that sometimes when we get to adulthood, we wonder who we really are. Who is the real me?

Sometimes we create so many different images of ourselves that we become mentally ill. The world of fantasy takes possession of us. We don't know where to find the "honest-to-goodness" me.

Does this mean, then, that the person who shouts when he is angry, who hits his brother when he sees him, who stays home from church when he feels like "the devil," who refuses to do the job his boss assigns him, who doesn't answer people when they greet him on the street is more honest than the one who tries to behave and cover up his true feelings of the moment?

What is the difference between the true integrity of a maturing individual who is developing into a real person, and the person who is creating a basically dishonest image of himself?

Each of us, when he is born, is given the potential to develop into a true person, into an honest person. But it is necessary to be able to tell the true from the false. Only someone who knows diamonds can tell a true diamond from a glass one. Only someone who knows arithmetic can tell a right answer from a wrong one. It is necessary to know someone who is true and who is honest in order to know what a true and honest person should be.

Only someone who starts with the truth can grow in that direction. Only someone who derives his understanding from a source that is without question a flawless source of light can find the honest illumination of all things.

The Christian believes that there is such a person, there is such a truth, there is such a light in Jesus Christ. When we start with this premise, we see ourselves in relationship to him. We know that we have drives and impulses that push us in many directions. We know that these impulses require control.

We know that the energy and drive within us needs to be harnessed. We know that if we give unbridled freedom to ourselves, we will trample on anything that gets in our way. We will destroy whatever tries to hamper us. Like the wild horse, we will plunge and rear and throw off the restraints of propriety. Yet, some people equate this freedom with being honest, with being true to oneself.

The Christian says something different. He says he was born a sinner, he was born to be dishonest, to cover up his true nature because he knows he is a sinner. Long, long ago with the birth of the story of Adam and Eve, when they hid from God in the garden, this kind of man knew wickedness and guilt.

To be completely honest, we must make this admission before we make any other. When we are completely honest about the kind of persons we are, then we have the power to become really honest about other things.

When we stand in church on Sunday morning and take part in the confessions of our sins, we expose ourselves to everyone around us for what we honestly are. When we take part in the Lord's Supper, we acknowledge before everyone that we are grateful to Jesus whose body had to be broken for us because we are not essentially honest or good. At that moment we present a true image of ourselves.

Once we have been honest about ourselves, we stand a good chance of being able to tell the honest word from the dishonest one, the honest act from the dishonest one.

When we try to keep our relationship with Jesus Christ alive through worship, study and prayer, we gain an understanding that makes it possible for us to write an honest story, or paint a true picture or act in a fantasy even though what appears to be fact is distorted. The underlying truth is there.

But it is easy to hide from God. It is easy to make up stories about ourselves that show us to be something we would like to be. It is easy to be dishonest once Jesus Christ is removed. And it is very easy to let him go. He passes away so quietly, not a breath is heard. Until suddenly we awake one day to find him gone.

With him gone, we no longer know who we honestly are. For as long as we were his creatures, we knew what we were. We knew who we were. For it is far better to be a sinner kneeling at Jesus' table for forgiveness, than to be a king with a scepter and throne who doesn't know the true from the false, the honest from the sham.

Honesty makes it possible for us to be forgiven sinners. Being forgiven sinners makes it possible for us to be grateful sons of God.

EVENING PRAYER

I don't usually do this but tonight I am going to make an inventory of my day.

Did I set aside any part of this day for prayer and meditation? I did not.

Did I once think about those less fortunate that I am to see how I could serve them? I did not.

Did I look at the world around me and find that I was filled with joy at my part in it? I did not.

Did I lose my temper? I did.

Did I get disgusted because I had to scrub my floor again so soon? I did.

No wonder I need to pray for forgiveness daily!

"Dear Lord I pray thee to forgive me for my sins this day. Help me to be renewed this night so that tomorrow may be an opportunity to begin again. In Jesus' name. Amen."

ON BEING CHASTE

Someone is snickering. That word. What does it mean?
To be chaste, to be pure.
To be a virile man, to be an ardent woman.
These two statements are contradictions, are they not?

Chastity is the subject for jokes. People don't want to talk about their indiscretions. But they don't want to be thought lacking them either.

A boy is expected to try out his virility in a sexual experience. A girl is advised that she, too, can find fulfillment in a sexual relationship. A boy and girl cannot be expected to have a warm, human affair without sexual experience.

To expect a person to restrain his sexual impulse is like expecting a mother to tie a young child to a post rather than to let the child walk about freely. Naturally it is better not to be too promiscuous. It is wise to show a little taste in one's affairs. One person at a time--maybe.

Is this the Christian point of view? No, it is not. The Christian idea is that a man and a woman share the sexual experience only in the marriage relationship.

But there is no area in which our culture shows how little this Christian idea means to men than this area; that is, if surveys are correct.

Why has the Christian church maintained what some people call such a rigid point of view?

Well, what is the purpose of sex? Is it to cause exciting sensations that are rather devastating, to say the least? Is it to release a certain amount of tension? Is it to give a cozy feeling of intimacy?

Much tragedy and sorrow have resulted when these were reasons for the unrestrained release of the sex impulse. What other reason would there be for its indiscriminate use?

Anyone who has experienced sex as it has been advocated by the Christian church all these many years has moments of unutterable sadness when he realizes what other people have missed in their mad dash for this ultimate experience that they never find. For once a person has had this experience, he knows he has had it. And he never looks for it anywhere else, for he knows he has had the ultimate in human relationship.

Little does the dashing man-about-town know what he is advertising about himself when he makes himself available to any attractive woman in sight. He has never had it. And the woman who preens herself for any man who happens to be about is acknowledging a devastating lack in her life.

What is this Christian view of sex? The marriage ceremony speaks for itself. These two shall become one flesh. A man shall leave his father and mother and cleave to his wife. These persons become part of each other. They pour themselves into each other. They achieve mutual happiness through a complete giving of self.

This is the only way that the sex act can reach its real climax, for there is a merging of two people that makes them actually become one. The physical delight is enhanced by the mutual esteem the two people have for each other. This is impossible without a love that is ready to control itself to meet the needs of the other person.

It is interesting how God's law of love works even in this instance. For it is only in the complete giving of oneself that this tremendous overflowing exalting feeling can come. Once it has come, there comes also the realization that there could never be more than this. That is why the person who is always looking reveals that this has not been true for him.

God has made sex of such a nature that only when it is used as he designed it does man achieve the totality of the sexual experience. All he gets the other way is a brief, fleeting, momentary sensation of physical desire satisfied. Sometimes he doesn't even get that.

To give oneself away to someone in the sexual act is to lose part of oneself. In the marriage relationship this works because someone gives you something in return. It is a continuous giving and receiving. But this also goes on in all one's other acts as well so that there is total union. When the relationship is only temporary, one gets drained of oneself to the point of genuine frustration.

The sad thing is that in obstructing God's way, man brings unhappiness to countless people. He often becomes obsessed with his sexual drives. He makes no effort to control them or to take an interest in anything else.

It is a matter of concern that Christians, rather than speak of the joy that comes with maintaining a chaste relationship, remain silent. Christians let sex become the property of the depraved, the dissatisfied, the profligate and the renegade. Their views become a part of our literature, our theater and our mores.

Young people grow up in a world where the only kind of sex they hear about is the sexual life of the non-Christian, the more unsatisfactory kind there is if the divorce courts, the number of unwed mothers and the sexual deviates are any indication.

If Christians have found the joy they should within the marriage relationship as God intended it, they could not stand by to watch young people being sold down the river by those people who consider the discipline of the sexual drive an archaic arrangement.

To be chaste, to be pure.

Virile men have been, ardent women have been. Happily so.

Chastity is a Christian virtue, and like all virtues, it is designed for man's good and not for his destruction.

EVENING PRAYER

Close your eyes. It's night.

I close them gladly. They are tired from the glare of lights and moving things they watch all day. My body is so tired from running around. I sink into the mattress to let the tired muscles rest. I bury my head into the pillow. I refuse to think about anything.

Only one thing I have left to do. I want to put my soul into God's hands, to set my mind completely at rest.

"Oh God, I let my soul rest in the hollow of thy hand where it may rest all the other weary souls who are entrusted to thee. May those restless souls who have not found the hollow of thy hand find thee soon. In Jesus' name. Amen"

ON BEING BORED

This is a silly subject for me to write about. I've never been bored in my life.

I've been angry, depressed, disgusted, pained, tired, irritated, but never bored.

I've been happy, gay, peaceful, contented, calm, but never bored.

When the question of eternal life comes up, I've heard people say, "I'd hate to live forever. What would you do? How boring to go on and on forever and ever!"

I stared at them in amazement. This is exactly what appeals to me about the whole thing. This is why Jesus' promise of eternal life in him makes response so credible. Imagine not being restricted by time. The thought is tremendous, overwhelming and altogether satisfying - no end to desire, understanding, or exploration.

The world which God has created is such a fascinating place, I never stop being surprised.

In fact, I am surprised all the time, just in my relationship with human beings. I think I can predict exactly how my husband, my children, my friends, my pastor will react to something. But they don't react the way I expect. They come up with a completely new kind of behavior. This always results in some new insight. Well, just think of all the people there are in the world, all of them with different reactions. I grow dizzy just thinking about knowing a few of them.

There is the matter of taste. I think I have fixed hamburger all the ways it is possible to fix it. Then someone brings a completely new dish to a picnic, prepared with hamburger, yet tasty, succulent, different.

Every time our family goes to a music shop to buy a record, there are new ones we have never heard before and some we would dearly love to own.

Each spring the smell of lilacs tantalizes me as if I had never smelled them before. That first rhubarb, fresh out of the cold moist earth that has hardly forgotten the feel of snow on it, has in it the flavor of the wild winter, sharp, tangy and new to the taste buds.

I sit at coffee with my friends. We have talked back and forth for years. Have we exhausted each other's minds so that there is nothing new to say? Indeed not. One evening someone puts a phrase together in a new way. It is funny. Everyone laughs. It inspires someone else to try to create another play on words. Soon everyone is laughing.

I expect that one hundred million good Christians with one accord will pounce on me - "This is not what is meant by eternal life-- new ways of eating hamburger, lilacs, delightful music and laughing conversation."

They think eternal life is a purely spiritual concept. It's about souls. Heaven is not a place where you can eat ice cream, or paint a picture or create a song.

But what is your soul? Does your soul exist apart from you? Does it have an existence of its own completely separate from you as you are now?

It is interesting that one of the definitions of the soul is that it is the breath of life. My soul is what gives meaning to my existence. It is the palpitating, breathing, zestful, invisible connection with the infinite. But these good things to eat, to see and to smell is my soul separate from these things? Is it floating in space somewhere apart from me?

I have become what I am because of the things I have seen or heard or felt. My soul is different from every other soul because no one else has seen or heard or felt exactly the same things that I have seen or heard or felt at the same time that I saw or heard or felt those things.

But I am coming to the thorny part of my little rhapsody, this pretty picture of eternal life that I have created where I can go on eating new foods, seeing new sights, hearing new sounds, meeting new people. This body that likes to do all these things is going to die. That breath of life is going to leave it.

That spark that animates conversation is going to be doused with the bitter water of death. I have seen its ugly presence many times. That laughing, sparkling person is no longer here. Those heartwarming, comforting hands are cold. They are gone.

This talking about souls after death is a ticklish business. I'm not qualified to do it. I'm just wondering about it out loud. I have the hope that God does not ruthlessly abandon my soul or anyone else's to the oblivion of death, that he does not drown my spirit in death's murky waters, that he does not cruelly quench forever that unborn spark of mine.

There is one person who has given me this hope, and that is Jesus Christ. And after him, Paul and Peter, John and Luke, the saints and Luther, and every pastor who has ever read the funeral service. Jesus has promised that every soul can have eternal life, and he has promised it right now.

However, there are many people who admit that they are bored with life. Many people get tired of living. Since God made this world, and they do not find it exciting, they naturally want to die. It is probably just as well. For whatever other worlds there are, God will have made them, too.

That is precisely why the Christian finds the thought of donning the garment of immortality given by Jesus Christ such a prized thing. He never exhausts the possibilities of this life, so he has hopes that it will continue on and on. He is sure that anything else that God would have in mind would be better and greater, for he has already experienced this life in Christ here.

This is the point, though. One's soul is formed and developed here and now in this environment of taste and sight and sound and thought. This is the moment for loving, for obeying and for delighting in God. If there is no thankfulness or joy or curiosity for what God has made, the soul--that flowering of the spirit--gets parched and shriveled like an apple left to rot in the cellar of boredom.

But who knows what happens to the soul that reaches, that stretches, that gravitates toward God. What happens to the soul that soars with curiosity beyond the limits of the body? Does that breath of life revive the same old body or does it take another form? Where will Jesus' gift of eternal life take us? What is the heaven that Jesus talks about? What does God have in mind?

It is exciting to think about, isn't it?

EVENING PRAYER

This day has ended, like many other days in which most of us worked and existed. To a few of us it was a special day but for most of us it was an ordinary day filled with ordinary things.

But are they ordinary? Can one say it is ordinary to move, to run, to speak, to eat? And to think, to imagine, to paint pictures in the mind?

If that is ordinary, I am very grateful for the ordinary.

"Oh God, who hast blessed me abundantly with the ordinary things, grant me an ordinary night's sleep. In Jesus' name. Amen."

ON BEING ALONE

THERE ARE many moments of the day when I am alone. The only person I talk to is myself. When the sun comes dancing through the window, casting flecks of light on my cut glass bowl, I see it alone. When the mist hides the world in gray gauze, I feel its soft coolness alone. When the dog barks down the street, I hear it alone.

I love to be alone--sometimes.

I see more, I hear more, and I feel more. Colors take on meaning, sounds are intensified and I become aware--of the green of the grass, the blue of the sky, the call of the meadowlark, the balmy breeze blowing my hair. I see pussy willows by the side of the road. I see a chipmunk scurry across my path. I hear the wind rustle the tall grass. I touch the down of a dandelion.

In the city when I am alone, I see more, too.

I see the people as they hurry by--the tense preoccupied look, the aimless "what shall I do now" look, the determined "I'll get what I want yet" look and the "laughing together" look.

I hear the motors hum, the bells clang, the feet shuffle, the whistles shrill in a blend of the sounds, not tranquil but not unpleasant.

I become aware, too, that many lives appear to be touched by the sordid, by the cheap and tawdry, by the artificial and extravagant, by the bitter and bleak, by the exciting and new.

But am I truly alone?

In my house, in the country, in the city, am I alone? I did not make myself. I do not keep myself going. The things I see, that I hear, that I feel are all there because someone else put them there. I cannot escape creation any more than I can escape myself. And I cannot escape God any more than I can escape myself. This life I have is a continual reminder of him. Even in my most complete aloneness, he is there. Those thoughts tucked deep in my brain are exposed to him. That nakedness I usually hide is seen by him.

I cannot ever really be alone.

But that is good, for although there are times when I like solitude, there are times when I hate it.

It is dreadful to wake up in the middle of the night alone when the world is black, my body is run down and I feel that no one cares.

It is dreadful to lie on a hospital bed, alone, waiting for the morning, for the operation, for the inevitable pain.

It is dreadful to watch a child's asthmatic breathing, alone, to be helpless to ease it.

It is dreadful to walk into a strange crowd of convivial friends, alone, not a familiar face.

It is dreadful to find the person I love does not love me, that I am alone in my feeling.

But I am mistaken. I am not alone.

I cannot ever really be alone.

For God not only enters my aloneness through creation. He enters it though the he love he has for this creation. He not only made me. He loves me. Because he loves me, he will not let me endure the pain, the bleakness, the helplessness alone. Though it does not always seem so, he is there.

There is no solitude, even in death.

We are made by God. We are his.

There is no way to evade him.

At times, this is a comfort.

At times, this is disconcerting.

At times, this is sheer joy.

But *always*, he is there with me.

EVENING PRAYER

Some people's nights are filled with sound--cars and trucks going endlessly by their windows, someone's hi-fi or radio or TV booming next door, a gang of unsupervised young people roaming through the streets by their home, trains chugging in the distance, planes whirring overhead.

My night is quiet. Where I live everyone goes to bed. We are off the beaten track--no cars, no trains, no planes. I have not always lived this way. Once I loved the noise and activity. Now I love peace and silence.

I suppose that is known as adaptation, this ability to become part of one's environment.

"Oh God, I thank thee for the place where I am. Yet, without thee this place, too, would be nothing. Let me never so lose my desire for thee that I could exist apart from thee. In Jesus' name. Amen."

ON BEING A STUDENT

One of the phrases I dislike to say is "I don't know."

To look at a piece of sculpture and to know nothing of its creation . . .

To hear a piece of music and to know nothing of its origin . . .

To go to a play and to know nothing of the background that caused it to be born . . .

To read a philosopher's work and to know nothing of the age in which he lived . . .

To hear a strange language and to understand not a single word . . .

To watch an astronaut whirling through space and to know nothing of what keeps him there . . .

All these fill me with curiosity, make me want to know and to be able to comprehend what I have seen.

Fortunately there are ways of knowing. There are libraries filled with books and periodicals. There are schools staffed with teachers. There are laboratories dedicated to knowing. All that is needed is the desire to know and the time to absorb it all.

I remember how it felt when I was a child in school when the teacher asked a question. Everyone in the class said, "I don't know," until she came to me and I knew. There would come the feeling that this curiosity of mine that had prompted my learning, it had its purpose.

It gives me a feeling of satisfaction when my child asks a question and for a change I do know the answer.

It is rewarding when I hear a sermon or a lecture to know what the man is talking about, to follow his line of reasoning, and to understand his illustrations because at one time I had learned something.

But a real student is always a student. There is no graduation for the real student. A real student is born with the desire to know. And since it is impossible to know all there is to know in one lifetime, a true student is always a student.

However, that is one of the joys of being a student, to know that I can never exhaust the supply of my delight.

I love that sensation of light dawning in my brain. It is like a rush of cool water clearing my mind to make room for this new sensation.

This joy of learning can be mine as long as I live, for God has made a world that is so vast in its scope that each person can find something new which he alone can contribute.

There is the world of words - what infinite combinations of them can be made!

There is the world of numbers, of music, of painting, of sculpture, of the theater, of the dance, of flowers, of birds, of rocks, of bugs, of mountains, of lakes, of people. It goes on and on.

There is another world, too.

To walk into a cathedral where the stained-glass windows divert the penetrating rays of the sun so that a sense of mystery prevails creates in me a curiosity to want to know what caused man to build this kind of structure as a part of worship.

To hear the loud sweeping strains of a cantata makes me want to ponder why the composer wanted to reveal the power of God in this way.

To walk through a hospital or a rest home or a home for crippled children makes me want to understand the necessity for suffering and the desire in people to alleviate it.

To read my morning paper with its endless accounts of murders, divorce, robberies, rape and evil makes me curious about man's nature and what could change it.

To sense my own finiteness, my own smallness, my own tendency to evil makes me want to know this world of the spirit.

This world is not seen, not comprehended by the eye or the ear or even the brain, and yet touches them all. It is that world of the spirit through which God speaks to us.

Even in this world I can be a student. There are things I can know about God, things revealed in Jesus Christ. As I grow, the revelation of these things becomes clearer. It becomes more infinite in its scope. Through the means of the natural world I gain understanding into this spiritual world at the same time I can never confine the spiritual world to the natural world.

But when, by being a student of the spirit, a new insight is given me, joy comes like the rush of a mighty wind to sweep me for a moment into touch with the infinite.

To be a student in God's world is the vocation of a lifetime.

EVENING PRAYER

Some nights my bed is such a haven.

I can flee there from the bustle and noise. I can get away from the questions to be answered. It is good to know that someone has enough faith in me to ask me questions, but the answering is hard. My brain aches with finding the right answer.

The tests I took as a girl in school were easy compared to the questions I am asked almost every day--moral and spiritual questions as well as academic ones. Yet each question for which I must find an answer has made me a more mature person.

"Dear Lord, I thank thee for my mind and its exercise, for the fascinating unexplored areas I sometimes find in it. Help me to find right answers and help me now to rest. In Jesus' name. Amen"

ON BEING GRACIOUS

Does the word "gracious" call to your mind the picture of women pouring tea, talking in purring tones, flowers on a lace cloth, perfume wafting through the air?

Or do you see a serene hostess extending her hand in warm hospitality as you enter the glass doors of a mansion?

Do you think of the word gracious only when you refer to women who behave as ladies should?

Actually this is a very shallow conception of the word gracious.

The word gracious is a word meaning much more than outward beauty and social poise, much more than breeding and good manners, much more than feminine artfulness.

Graciousness has deep roots. Good manners are only the leaves that merely dress the tree.

Graciousness is the art of giving oneself. It is bestowing oneself on the other person. It is a giving of kindness. It comes from knowing that giving oneself is a worthy gift.

Ungracious people are the ones who have not found any worth within themselves to bestow. They are taciturn, brusque, rude, or belligerent because they are displeased with what they have found themselves to be. They have nothing to give to other people.

Wealth is not the answer. There are many millionaires who are not gracious, and many poor people who are.

This quality of graciousness comes from the person who is rich in spirit. He feels an abundance within himself that he wants other people to feel. He reaches out toward other people. He moves toward them. He doesn't hold himself back with diffidence. He meets his fellow men with a sense of affluence. He has something that makes him feel like a man, that makes him feel good, that makes him recognize that there is something that he has to give.

The gracious person can afford to be gracious because he knows that someone has been very gracious to him. He has found the great source of graciousness. He has found God.

But not only has he found God. He is very glad that he has found him. God to him is not a restrictive, outmoded, formidable, demanding, liturgically correct kind of irritant.

God to him is real and gracious--full of love, kindness, sympathy, righteousness, generosity, purity and compassion.

God is the cool clean well from which he gets the water of life for his spirit. God has entered into him and cleaned him. He is a human being who knows that God loves him. That is his secret. For no matter how poor he is, no matter how plain he is, no matter how inept he is, no matter how lowly is his station in life, he can still be gracious. He is not ashamed of himself. God has made him not ashamed. He can always be the gentleman - beneficient, courteous, considerate, outgoing.

Why, then, are there not more gracious people when God has been so generous with his love toward us all?

God bestows his love graciously but man must also accept it graciously. He must acknowledge that it is a gift. He has not earned it and he has not deserved it. His efforts do not change the quality of the gift. The only thing he can do with the gift is to share it.

For to be gracious is actually an obligation from the one who has accepted God's graciousness. It requires a bestowing of oneself for others, a giving of oneself. One cannot just pretend to be nice and generous. One must actually be it.

As God so freely gives, so must his benefactors. The man who feels worthy in himself feels worthy only when he knows that God has made him that way. Any other kind of worth that a man feels is sheer sham. God has made each man and God is the only one who can make a man feel his true worth. And unless he feels worthy in the way in which God wants him to feel worthy, then that man is a hypocrite and is unable to feel gracious.

It is interesting that the Christian has so often been pictured as the retiring, quiet, unworthy, pallid, inhibited, shrinking kind of person.

It is a picture drawn by a person who has not known God. For knowing God gives a man dignity, respect, poise, backbone and worthiness.

Christianity was not spread by men who were retiring, afraid, and quiet.

It was spread . . .

By humble men who had been given something of which to be proud;

By poor men who had been given something that made them act like the richest of men,

By illiterate men who had been given something that made them able to preach to the wise.

God is gracious. Are you?

EVENING PRAYER

Restful is a soothing word. That is what night is, something to soothe tired bodies, restless nerves, weary minds.

But the coming of night alone cannot do this. My spirit needs something more than the mere physical appearance of night - the darkness, the stars, the quiet. My spirit needs the benediction of the Almighty to bring me rest.

"O Lord, bless and keep me. Make thy face to shine upon me, and give me peace. In Jesus' name. Amen."

ON BEING FEARFUL

To be is to fear.

To see a huge wave swelling from the sea cresting with frothy force before it hits the beach where I am standing makes me feel fear.

To watch orange tongues of fire licking the prairie grass with greedy gulps as it sweeps toward me makes me feel fear.

To observe black clouds rolling and seething with angry winds as they plunge toward the earth where I am makes me feel fear.

To be on a boat that is blindly feeling its way through white wispy impenetrable fog while horns toot forlornly all about me makes me feel fear.

To walk along a wooded path at night while leaves whisper about me and things fly before me and something crawls near me makes me feel fear.

To stand on a subway platform alone looking down the eerie tunnel for a train that never comes while an unshaven, unkempt man, the only other person, lurches and stumbles near me makes me feel fear.

I could go on.

My world is full of fearful things.

If what I have read and heard and observed is true, I am not alone in being fearful. It has been a common human characteristic through the ages. It is present in a man from his birth to his death.

It would be good to be able to say that fear grows less as I grow older. It is one of the things that I can conquer. But it would not be true. I can conquer one fear only to have another take its place. What I feared as a child seems trivial to what I fear now.

It is even worse. For as a child my mother's soft arms and my father's confident words made fear disappear satisfactorily. They stood between me and my fears.

Not any more! I stand alone with that clutching, strangling enemy of mine.

Now is the time to blithely say, "You are not alone. God is there."

That is true. God is there.

But God does not stand between me and my fears.

God is not going to snatch me away from the operating table when the surgeon gets ready to inflict pain on me.

God is not going to deflect that airplane on which I am riding if it starts hurtling toward the earth because of some mechanical difficulty.

God is not going to take the radiation from the hydrogen bombs and turn it into harmless dew.

God does not send a sparkling white angel to perch on my son's bicycle as he rides to school or to whisper in my daughter's ear as she drives our car down the freeway.

God makes me look at my fears.

It seems to me that to say that God will take away my fear is to try to turn a dream world in which there is no fear into a reality. It would be trying to live in a world which I have created and not to live in the world which God has created.

And the world which I would create, a world where there could be no fear, would not be a real world at all. It would be a sham, an illusion, a mirage. I cannot create a world for I am not God.

I must live in the world which God has made, if I am to live at all. It is a world in which there is danger on every hand. It is a world in which there is struggle and difficulty, but it is the only real world there is.

The only way to face fear is to live the fact that it will always be there, for I have seen it in the faces of the very old as well as the very young.

I will never be able to wake up in the morning and say, "Well, there is nothing to be afraid of today." I'd be kidding myself.

Instead, I must be willing to admit that any of these things could happen.

At the same time, I must admit that God is good for I have seen his goodness. He is merciful, for he has shown it in every generation. He has shown it to me. He is love, for he has created love, that force without which life is unbearable. And I have tasted that love.

So while I must face the fact of my fears, I must also face the fact that God is love.

This does not take away my fears, but it helps me to live with them.

For God did not create a world of pillows. He created one of rocks, and seas, and winds and earth.

God did not make marshmallows. He made nuts in shells, hard crackling apples hanging high on trees, and potatoes deep in the soil waiting to be dug.

God made a world in which I must struggle to survive, struggle with nature, with other people, with my inner self.

There is never a time when I win this struggle. But as long as I keep struggling, I never lose either.

Even the gift of God's love, this love that helps me live with my fear, comes to me with an element of struggle in it. I have to struggle with my pride that doesn't want to admit that it is only by God's grace I have the strength to struggle.

But it helps just to know that this is the way things are. It helps to know that there is one who went before me who knew the power of that struggle to the very end when he cried with a loud voice, "My God, my God, why hast thou forsaken me!"

But God had not forsaken Jesus, and he has not forsaken me.

EVENING PRAYER

I wonder if I glowed today

I'm afraid there were times when the light of my love flickered very faintly. I became concerned only with myself and my house. I put my interest above the interest of others.

I let worry and anxiety overwhelm the brilliant light of love with dark and foreboding clouds.

"Forgive me, oh Lord, for letting my trust in thee waver and become obscure, for letting the cares and irritabilities of little things take precedence over the greatness and strength of thy love and compassion. Enter into my heart this night to keep my mind on thee and to refresh my soul with thy Spirit. In Jesus' name. Amen."

ON BEING A SINNER

Sin! There the word stands--isolated, alone, bold.

To some, sin is a provocative word. It is the brightness and lights of a gaudy stage. It is the tantalizing challenge of the gambling table. It is a joust in which one dances and parries with a formidable devil who taunts a person into taking him on all alone.

To some sin is a repulsive word. It is the diseased body of an old prostitute. It is the drunk slobbering in the gutter. It is a force that pulls a person with it down into a quicksand of disease, filth and stench.

To some sin is an archaic word. It is a word that was once used to express maladjustment. It describes antisocial behavior. It has sometimes indicated the individual who refused to conform. To these people sin is a word for which man is not responsible. As such, sin no longer has any meaning, for since man is the product of an environment whose forces have made him what he is, he cannot be said to sin.

To some, sin is a bitter word. It is the rift that left an old parent to die unforgiven. It is the divorce between two quick-tempered people. It is the end of a long friendship. It is the long silence that holds the tongue paralyzed when just a word would heal. It is the endless nightmare of guilt that makes peaceful slumber an impossibility.

To me sin is real, harsh, ugly.

It is a provocative word because it taunts me every day to do or to be that which I know is not right.

It is a repulsive word because so often I hate myself when I know I've been in its grasp, if only for a while.

It is an old word because I have known its destructive action all my life, even as a child.

It is a bitter word because it has caused me to say things which I have longed to take back.

Sin never lets me alone. To me, sin is the personification of evil for it seems to try to possess me as if I were some prize painting, which I am not! My sublimest moments are so very brief only because sin is there leering, grinning, and trying, often with success, to spoil perfect occasions.

Sin is what keeps me knowing God only partially. It tries always to sully those moments when prayer seems most meaningful, when worship is most inspiring and when contemplation is most profound.

Sin is what keeps the face of God always overshadowed with a cross. I cannot shout with joyful abandon, "Hallelujah, Jesus saved me!"

Of course he saved me. But at what cost! The fact that it was necessary at all tempers any unalloyed joy. For though there is joy, there is also a sense of indebtedness that makes me want to whisper, "For me this painful ordeal was necessary."

That is something I don't feel like shouting, especially when I have to come back to him constantly asking forgiveness, because, like the little child, my hand is constantly in sin's cookie jar and I am tempted to taste and to consume.

When I use the word sin, I mean that thing in me that makes me put my own desires before everything else, that thing that makes me lack pity for others, that thing that takes away my courage in the face of difficulties, that thing that makes me lose my trust in God, that thing that makes me envy even those I love, that thing that makes me give excuses for not doing acts of charity.

Isn't that sin? What else would you call it?

Sin is always with me. But so is God. And when things are at their worst, God comes and towers over me. Then sin shrivels and slithers away, for the time being. It always comes back. That is why I must admit I have to make constant use of the means God has given me to keep contact with him. For being a sinner, I truly do need him.

EVENING PRAYER

Over and over again I climb into bed weary of my failures, tired of my tasks, fatigued by the spread of my activities.

But when sleep comes with its state of unconsciousness, energy stores up, spirits brighten, interest is kindled, and I wake refreshed.

"Oh God, I thank thee for sleep's healing powers. I thank thee for these hours of forgetfulness. At the same time, I am glad that thou dost have no need for sleep, that thou dost not forget me. Watch over us this night and always. In Jesus' name. Amen."

ON BEING GLIB

A woman feels taut, edgy, distraught. She cries if her husband goes out bowling with the boys. She cries when her children talk back to her. She can't stand to walk through a crowded department store. She can't stand anything. She feels miserable.

Yet there seemingly is nothing wrong with her. What can she do?

She can pray. But she has prayed all her life. She has never stopped.

She can turn to Jesus. But she has. She has cried to Him as she has to everyone else.

She has heard all the glib phrases that come so readily from the mouths of Christians. Turn to Jesus. Read the Psalms. Pray to God. Have faith.

A man loses interest in his job. He lies awake at night tossing and turning. What is the point of it all? His wife is always wanting something, not just things money can buy. She wants him. She wants his company. Sometimes he would just like to be left alone. His children irritate him. He doesn't feel like playing ball or being ridden like a horse. Food tastes like sawdust. He snaps at his co-workers. Why is he so discontented?

He has heard all the glib answers, too.

He goes to church as he always has. He listens to the preacher. He prays and it feels like talking into cotton until he feels suffocated by it.

The teen-ager suddenly feels overwhelmed with futility, tired of trying to keep up with the crowd, strangely alone even with the family all around, unable to study and to concentrate.

He, too, tries out the things he has been told so glibly. He prays, and he feels nothing. Where is God? He goes to Luther League, the same frenetic crowd only they sing hymns instead of something else.

Too many Christians give too many glib answers to tormented souls. More than one person has been lost because a Christian knew all the answers.

They were so easy. Just try Jesus. Have faith. Pray. Trust in God.

So they try all of these. They read about Jesus. They try to pray. They try to have faith. But nothing helps.

Now they really despair. Why isn't God helping them? Why doesn't Jesus come to them? What is wrong with their faith? Is it true that for some reason God no longer loves them--perhaps he never has?

Blackness comes in upon them like a shroud. They are ready to quit the struggle and give up. Many of them do. Some die. Some drink. Some try one doctor after another. Some try to find themselves by developing an interest in art or music or politics. But they have no peace, no joy in living, no feeling of purpose or worthiness either in themselves or in anyone else. They are willing to seek if they know where to seek.

Does life have meaning and purpose? Of course it has.

Is joy to be had in living? Of course it is.

Do I count for anything? Of course I do.

But where do I find this? In Jesus? In prayer? In faith?

Yes, it can be found in all three, but there is no magic about any of them. Jesus does not wipe away problems with a tear or a drop of his precious blood. Prayer does not illuminate the mind with a great spotlight that blots out all the wrong answers and shows up the right ones. Faith is no good luck charm that takes the danger and the difficulties out of living.

There is nothing that will do this. It is a shock to have to face up to this. But no one knew it better than Jesus. He knew what he was going to have to face--scorn, pain, uncertainty, loneliness and death. Nor did he promise his followers anything less.

Jesus was a realist. He faced facts exactly as they were. He never evaded them. He knew there was evil. He knew there was pain and sorrow in living. He knew his disciples would have to face problems just as we have to face them.

Prayer can be a comfort, but real prayer can also be a struggle, almost a torment, as a man presents himself before God, as he tries to analyze himself before God, as he reveals himself to God.

Faith is being willing to step out, often in the darkness on no sure road. It is a winding road that gives no clear view of the future. No man knows what is around the bend. He only knows that Jesus has walked it before him and that there actually is a road.

But it is strange. Once a person acknowledges to himself that there is no magic formula to solve problems, no easy way to overcome difficulties, no promise of the future being any easier, he finds Jesus not so hard to understand. He finds himself praying spontaneously, and he finds faith an adventure in living.

Each day is a gift. Perhaps there will be an answer to that problem today. But if there is not, he will still work at it. And he knows he must find the answer himself. No one will do it for him, not the psychiatrist, nor the professor nor the pastor. He knows that the answer is somewhere inside himself. And as he digs around, he begins to see what Jesus has been trying to say to him.

There is a curious exhilaration in making such discoveries. That child-like quality of joy in learning something new returns.

Now he sees new dimensions to life he had not noticed when he was so desperately trying to find an easy, pleasant way to amble through life. He gains new stature in his own eyes. God expects a great deal from him. God expects him to come through his difficulties. God expects him to find answers. And if God expects that of him, God knows that he can do it.

He knows, too, that solving one problem is not going to solve them all. There are always new ones to face. But instead of trying to avoid the problem or put it off on someone else, he tackles it himself.

Maybe this is just what is needed to make a return to joy in living possible. For joy is truly one of the chief ingredients of the Christian life.

And Jesus, instead of being some kind of Aladdin in a mythical tale, becomes the brother who has walked the same road on the same earth with the same kind of people we are.

EVENING PRAYER

It is dark again.

It is good to have everything hidden for a while, to have no distractions.

But my mind plays tricks on me.

Though there is nothing my eyes can see, my mind keeps flashing pictures of things I haven't done which I should have done, of things I wish I hadn't done which I have.

Though everything is silent around me, the loud speakers in my mind refuse to be silent. They keep blaring the things I have said over and over and I realize they were not gems of wisdom.

"Oh Lord, as thou hast hidden the world around us and made silent thy creation, so bid my mind to be quiet. Still the clamor that arises from my mistakes. Help me to empty my mind so that it can be filled with new ideas and kind thoughts that come from a night spent under thy love. In Jesus' name. Amen."

ON BEING A TROUBLEMAKER

Here's one that doesn't apply to you.

If there's anything you hate, it is to stir up trouble. When there is gossip among your neighbors, you try to change the subject. When there is controversy at your circle meeting, you keep still.

When someone questions the budget set up for your congregation, you quickly make a motion to have it passed to avoid arguments. When a petition of some sort is sent around, you put off signing your name if you can.

When your newspaper distorts the true picture, you would never think of writing a letter of protest. When someone suggests that a change of program might be stimulating, you quickly come to the defense of the status quo.

You don't want to hurt anyone. You don't want trouble.

Neither do I! I sit in my little house trying to be friends with everyone. I avoid meetings where decisions have to be made, stands have to be taken or people have to be told off.

You and I certainly are not troublemakers.

But I wonder if being a troublemaker is a thing always to be avoided. Let's think of some troublemakers.

Martin Luther	Abraham Lincoln
Elizabeth Fry	Louis Pasteur
Patrick Henry	Savonarola
Florence Nightingale	Anne Hutchinson

The list could be endless, and you would no doubt recognize them all. They were people who stirred up trouble. They were people who were hurt and threatened. They gave up contentment and ease. They risked reputation and safety. They fought the status quo.

They knew there was something worse than trouble. False religion, injustice, slavery, ignorance, crime, poverty, despotism, disease, are all worse than trouble.

These people are all dead. They fought the good fight.

But there are people today who are stirring up trouble. They carry placards. They write letters, organize protest meetings, get their names in the paper. Their friends avoid them. Their families needle them. Their jobs stand in jeopardy.

The thought of carrying a placard would send me promptly to bed with a migraine or a chill or diarrhea. How can people do it? How can they stir up so much trouble, not only for others, but also for themselves?

What gives them the courage, the drive, the conviction?

Maybe they have read the Bible. Maybe they have heard about Peter and Paul, Jeremiah and Isaiah, Timothy and Titus--great troublemakers!

Maybe they know Jesus, the greatest troublemaker of them all. He came to fight sin and to love sinners. Anyone who fights sin is unpopular with the sin-lovers. Anyone who loves sinners is unpopular with the sin-haters. Jesus did both.

And anyone who follows him is bound to be a troublemaker. We live in a world that is full of sin and sinners. If justice is to be done, poverty to be defeated, disease to be fought, slavery to be erased, righteousness to be revived, a person is bound to run into trouble.

But these are just concepts. What are the specifics? In your little nook, how can you get into trouble?

Frequently in communities there are things being done in schools that shouldn't be done or there are things that should be done that aren't. Frequently in cities, the government needs a thorough inspection to expose graft and corruption.

Sometimes in churches, there are budgets set up to be blindly accepted without adequate understanding on the part of the congregation. Some communities have mental hospitals, homes for the aged, or prisons that need to be examined for treatment to the inmates. Many towns need funds to carry on an adequate social agency for the misfits and the person who finds he can't win in his particular milieu.

Are you willing to be a troublemaker, the one who stirs people up?

Most communities have delinquent boys or girls "in trouble." Every city has its mental defectives, its parolees, its drug addicts, its drunkards. Every town has its poorly disciplined, poorly provided for families, its peculiar characters.

Are you willing to take the trouble to love them?

Being a troublemaker is not to be despised. Maybe it is a shame to say you are not one.

EVENING PRAYER

Have you ever felt the soft pads of a kitten's foot when the claws are carefully drawn back?

Their softness makes me think of the softness of night as it pads quietly, stealthily, but caressingly across the years. This night came that way. Now that it has come I want to hide in its darkness. The endless decisions that have to be made all day have worn me out. With each one is always the question--was my decision right or not?

To be concerned about the morality of something seems to be essential to being a person of integrity. I cannot see how one can make a decision frivolously. At the same time, once the decision has been made, the burden of it should pass away. It is a useless waste of energy to live through its making again.

"Oh God, please enlighten my mind to make right decisions and to accept the results of decisions already made. In Jesus' name. Amen."

ON BEING HAPPY

Am I writing this because I am so happy I'm bubbling like soapsuds?

Or because I'm so filled with joy that I can hardly keep my fingers still enough to write?

Or because smiles are curling my lips into expressions of delight?

No indeed. Quite the contrary.

Actually just now I'm so sad, so depressed, so frustrated, I can hardly stand it.

I wish I were happy. I wish I were bubbling. I wish I were smiling. But I'm not.

I'm sad, and I look it.

Maybe I have reason to be. Perhaps I've had a big disappointment, an unpleasant incident, moments of pain or nerves, unfair accusations or sad news.

Maybe the reason I'm so unhappy is that I know what it feels like to be happy.

I do. I love the feeling. When I have it, I clutch it and cling to it and am determined never to let it go. But it is an elusive thing. Suddenly it is gone. And I am curiously empty.

Actually circumstances don't seem to have too much to do with it. What makes me happy one time doesn't make me happy another. Usually my husband's presence is enough to make me happy, but sometimes I just wish he'd get out of the house! Sometimes I can laugh at almost anything. Other times no comedian on earth can get a flicker of a grin out of me. Sometimes I can turn my children's ill humor into laughter. Other times I scream at them and make it all the worse. We end up crying.

What makes me happy? What makes me unhappy?

Of course, sometimes it is just a matter of getting some sleep or taking a pill or breathing some fresh air.

But it is not all body chemistry.

There must be more to it than that.

Perhaps happiness is more than a feeling. Perhaps it is an attitude. A feeling is something rather spontaneous. I have very little control over my feelings. But my attitudes can be cultivated. They can be nourished by thoughts. They can be changed by words. They can be determined by will.

What is my attitude toward my husband? I want him to act toward me as if I were perfect, but I'm not.

What is my attitude toward my children? I want them to do exactly as I say when I say it, as if they were my property. But they are not.

What is my attitude toward my friends? I want them to find me so scintillating they wouldn't think of a party without me, but I'm not and they don't.

What is my attitude toward my work? I want to have the cleanest, shiniest house with very little effort. I want to be complimented every time I serve a good meal. I want to be recognized for being an excellent committee woman, a dependable leader and a writer of skill. I shudder when I write these down, but I'm afraid this is what I expect. And, of course, I'm not.

What is my attitude toward God? I want him to love me with a human rather than a divine love. I want to nestle in his arms, to be protected from all life's hurts, to be soothed and quieted. I want to be able to coax and wheedle him into doing all I want. And if I can't get it that way, I want him to hear my stormy pleas, wild cries, my stamping feet, my desperate outburst. I want him to see how I suffer. But he doesn't.

Well, what's wrong with my attitude?

Easy, isn't it? It shows up like a long dress at a tennis party, like a sour pickle in a dish of candy.

I am what is wrong with my attitudes. I have a very strong ego. It's very visible. I deserve to be unhappy with those attitudes.

It's curious. Until I wrote them down, I didn't realize how bad they actually were.

But I think I do know better. After all there are many times when I have been happy. Looking back, I'm quite sure they were the times when I abandoned myself and got lost in the enjoyment of the bright sunshine, the crisp air; the delightful knowledge of pleasing my husband and children; the gaiety that comes in a group of friends where no one is trying to impress anyone else; the sheer creativity of brightening the house with flowers, or clean curtains, or fresh linen; the glory of worshiping a God whose divine love can penetrate even my heart.

Just knowing what my attitudes are can help me to change them. If I change my attitudes because I want to be happy, I might be disappointed. If I change my attitudes because I realize that they are wrong, there's a chance some happiness might pounce on me unaware when I least expect it. That bubbling feeling that rises like a spring to refresh my soul comes. It must come from God.

Only he could create something so perfect as happiness.

EVENING PRAYER

Night has come.

I lie in my bed feeling contented tonight. This is not always the case. Sometimes I lie here so frustrated by things that have happened I can't sleep, and it takes me a long time to pray.

It has not been a great day, but it has been a day when I have felt that I have fulfilled my calling. My calling is not an unusual one that people write books about. It is simple and often menial, but my work has to be done and when I feel that I am the one called to do it, I can feel contented.

So, with a thankful heart, I pray.

"Dear Father in heaven, I have felt thy presence with me this day. It has brought me a serenity that has helped me to be a better member of my family and a more cheerful neighbor. Refresh me this night so that the day coming may be also a day of fulfillment. In Jesus' name. Amen."

ON BEING GENEROUS

I am writing this to make you feel good. I think that you'll feel that you are a generous person when you get through reading about me.

I am not generous at all. I hang on to everything I get. When I see the word "stewardship," little red flags start waving in my brain. I can feel my blood pressure rising. I know what that word means. It means I am supposed to give something.

I pretend it is that particular word I do not like. But actually it is the whole idea. I resist any sermon, or tract, or article on stewardship.

When I was a little girl I saved everything. Nothing of mine was broken, and nothing was shared, unless my mother made me do it. At Christmastime my mother would make me little cookies to put in my little tins to have for tea parties. I am sure I was the only child in town who still had some of those cookies left in her tins when Easter came.

When I was a teen-ager, I would go into New York City with a friend. She would say to me, "You are the only person I know who can go to New York and come home with more money than you took!" (slight exaggeration).

I could not see paying several dollars at some unusual restaurant when I could eat a roll and milk at the automat for very little. I could not see riding a bus or taxi ten blocks when I could walk. I could not see going to Radio City Music Hall in the afternoon when I could go there more cheaply in the morning. I would always look in the shop windows and dream of the day when I would have enough money to buy what I wanted. But I never bought anything.

I shall never forget one of my first dates with my husband. He bought orchestra seats to see Paul Robeson in "Othello." At the time he was wearing a threadbare overcoat and he still owed seminary debts. My niggardly soul literally shook. But it was a memorable performance. We had a wonderful time. And I think a spark of love got fanned into a flame that evening!

When I became a housewife, I judged other people's appetites by my own which was never very large. I would dish up one porkchop per person, one roll, one helping of vegetables, just enough salad and dessert. If anyone arrived unexpectedly at mealtime, I could never ask them to sit down and share with us. There was nothing left to share. No one ever groaned from having eaten too much when he got up from my table.

Now, I would like to be able to salve my conscience by saying this is just being thrifty. Surely saving money is a virtue.

Is it?

Benjamin Franklin might say, "Think of saving as well as getting. Be frugal and free."

But Benjamin Franklin is not my mentor. Jesus Christ is. And Jesus Christ never said, "For age and want save, while you may, no morning sun lasts a whole day."

Jesus said very odd things about saving, not at all practical or sensible or comfortable. At least not for me. "He who would save his life must lose it."

It would be a lot simpler to follow Benjamin Franklin's advice, don't you think?

That is the trouble with Jesus. He really upsets me. I know he wants me to be willing to take the shirt off my back--oh indeed, more than that, he wants me to be willing to share my house, my car, my hospitality with those who need it. He does not ask me just to put $5 or $10 or $100 in the envelope every Sunday morning. I can fit a certain amount for Sunday into my budget all right, and still save something.

But Jesus wants me to be ready to give and to share *all* that I am and *all* that I have without counting the cost.

Maybe this upsets you, too. Maybe you are not as generous as you thought you are.

If that's the case, why not give up this upsetting man, Jesus?

I cannot do that either, can you?

I would rather be upset by Jesus, even though I know he is probably going to turn me upside down and shake all those pennies out of my pockets, than to walk into the richly carpeted inner sanctum of the oldest bank in America to be told that the interest on my savings would take me around the world.

There is something about this man that gets through even my stingy crust. He possesses something that money cannot buy, and that I have seen in no one else. And it is something that he will not give me if I try to keep it for myself. The love that Jesus gives is not exclusive and cannot be hoarded. Its value cannot be measured. I only know it is the most valuable thing that could ever come into my life.

And I do not want to lose it - and yet if I am not willing to give it up, I will lose it. See how my stingy nature comes in again. I want to keep it. I want to save it, I want to be sure I hang on to it.

Even here, this man upsets me. It's not only money I have to share. I have to share love as well. Jesus loves me, but he loves all those other people, too. If my love for Jesus does not include them as well, I am only fooling myself. I no longer possess Jesus' love. I only possess my own love. And that kind of love turns sour and becomes vinegar the longer I have it.

But the very good thing about this Jesus is that he wants me just as much as he wants anyone else. So he keeps needling me and he keeps reminding me and he never lets me get away as long as I try to keep in touch with him. So if you ever notice any spurt of generosity on my part, you know that he has gotten through to me again.

EVENING PRAYER

Today was busy, busy, busy.

I love thee, Oh night, for coming to my rescue--to make my weary body rest, my active mind to slow down and my soul to be quiet. I can't go to sleep immediately. It takes the spinning wheels a while to stop.

But let me be serene as I lie here waiting for that tranquil moment that comes to bring sleep.

I can be calm as I pray to a God who knew what it was to rest and who saw that his work was good.

"Oh God, I thank thee for revealing some of thyself to us, for letting each of us know thee as a loving Father. I know thee as no one else can, and so does every other person. Thou art a God of wonder. In Jesus' name. Amen."

ON BEING CASUAL

Do you like proper people--people who always seem to do the right thing at the right time in the right place; women who always wear hats to church, who carry gloves automatically; men who never remove their coats anywhere except in the bedroom?

Or do they sometimes appear to you to be pompous?

Do you prefer the casual kind--the kind who always do what is most comfortable without any restraints, women who wear shorts for shopping, men to whom a tie is something to hang on a rack?

Our culture seems to lean toward the casual, don't you think?

In more ways than attire!

From what I read, apparently many men and women are just as casual about sleeping with one another as others are about drinking coffee together.

From what I hear, people are just as casual about swearing as children are about repeating nursery rhymes.

From what I have observed, students are just as casual about cheating as they are about drinking Cokes.

From what I have seen in statistics, it is evident people are just as casual about producing children as they are about having a hamburger at a drive-in.

From sad personal experience, it would appear that people are as casual about lying as they are about saying, "Good morning."

I've been thinking about this because I'm the casual kind of person.

As soon as I get in the house, I'm out of my dress and into my slacks.

At home I sit in my armchair with my legs plopped over one side.

I set an informal table, serve very informally, people helping themselves as much as possible.

I invite people to my house at the drop of a hat. "Come over for coffee in a few minutes."

I whisk the dustcloth over the furniture, pop something into the oven and put the coffee on.

I like casual living and I think I probably take pride in being that way.

But now I am beginning to have second thoughts on the subject. Maybe this casual living is just another word for easy living, the easy way to get by.

Maybe this casual attitude toward decorum and morality is just a way of showing indifference. Does it arise from a lack of conviction that there is a right way and a wrong way?

Or does it come because a person no longer cares about living the right kind of life?

Could one be so casual about adultery, swearing, cheating and lying if he felt it was wrong?

It takes effort to do things the right way. It takes discipline to plan, to study and to prepare. It takes a deepening of insight to use one's sex to fulfill a relationship rather than to achieve sensual satisfaction for oneself.

Perhaps living is like climbing a mountain. It takes effort to get to the top. There is only one way to climb, and that is by using one's strength with purpose. From the top, earth appears much grander and lovelier and heaven is within reach.

But one cannot be casual about climbing a mountain. One's life depends upon adequate preparation. It depends upon using one's body skillfully. It depends upon discovering what the terrain is and how best to cross it.

One cannot be casual about living either if one plans to get to the top. Life has to have a purpose and a direction. It has to have meaning. And to find the meaning for one's life requires endless searching and study. There is no easy way out.

One cannot find that meaning by cheating and trying to find the answer someone else has found in his life. For each one's life has its own peculiar meaning for its existence.

Men have helped each other by devising rules. When a person tries to live by these rules, he develops an understanding of their usefulness and their value for society.

As their meaning grows on him, he becomes less casual about obeying or not obeying them. For he understands that the rules were made by men who had climbed to the top, by men who had seen the whole vista of life.

For once a man gets the urge to climb the mountain and reach the top, nothing else will satisfy him. His life has purpose and meaning, and he knows what he wants.

That is why the Christian cannot be casual about life. He is concerned. He has a goal. Every nerve and fiber in his being stretches toward this goal. Anything that keeps him from this upsets him, worries him, concerns him. And he knows the rules. They are all set out before him.

He isn't casual about these rules, not at all. He cannot see them ignored without protest. They are the structure of his life, more important to him than anything else. They are what help him to climb the mountain.

And climbing he is, every day. He has a goal, an ambition, a purpose. He wants to know God. That is what dominates his life.

Have you ever tried to be casual about God?

I don't think that God will let you.

For God is a force that sweeps, that pulls, that tugs, that strains, that takes a person from a reclining position to stand squarely on his feet and to move him. There's nothing casual about God. He expects you to obey him, to serve him and to move at his command. No indifference is sanctioned by him.

And if by chance you feel casual about God, cry aloud, "Oh God, don't pass me by. Find me. Take me. Don't leave me here alone."

For if you are casual about him, it really means that you have never met him.

EVENING PRAYER

Tonight I am going to bed before I am ready for it. This is most unusual but it does happen sometimes. Everyone else has gone to bed and so have I. But I feel wide awake, my mind is racing down new paths. I want to write the thoughts down, but they are too elusive, like the constantly changing clouds on a bright windy day. The formations never stay still long enough to be described.

As I lie here, though, I think a measure of calm would come if I would close my eyes to pray.

"Dear Father in heaven, thou didst rest on the Seventh Day. If that great creative energy of thine could rest, thou wilt be able to make my mind rest. Help me to feel the quietness that must have come after thy great creation--the quietness of a baby's soft breath, a lily lying on a pool, or the velvet padding of a kitten's foot. In Jesus' name. Amen."

ON BEING A HATER

I heard a minister say over the radio the other day, "In order to be able to love, one must also be able to hate."

Startled, I stopped mopping my floor and stood there leaning on the mop handle. I felt as if someone had just handed me a cold glass of iced tea with mint in it on a hot day.

I listened some more. He mentioned words like loathe and abhor. He made it sound good to be able to loathe and abhor.

My brain started dancing around. "This is great, this is great!" it kept repeating as it whirled around.

There are quite a few things I loathe. I don't just dislike them. That is too mild a word. I really loathe them. At the same time, I feel guilty about loathing them. I get carried away by my emotions. For example:

I loathe cigars. But I love a wonderful father who smoked them.

I loathe crowds. But I love people.

I loathe cocktails. But I love parties.

I loathe suggestive movies and plays. But I love funny stories, even sexy ones.

I loathe boating. But I love the sea.

Of course, this is not what this particular minister was talking about, someone's private hates or loves.

He was saying, "Abhor evil--loathe that which is not good."

Don't be indifferent to it. Don't turn your head the other way just to avoid it. Don't become reconciled to it. *Loathe* evil, *abhor* evil, *hate* evil.

Hatred is a devastating, terrible passion. It can consume that at which it is directed.

I have watched mobs consumed by hatred. In minutes what were once human beings became savage animals. Their faces changed. Their voices changed. Their bodies reeked and churned. With intense cruelty they destroyed people and property.

This is a passion of which you and I are capable. We can be aroused to this kind of feeling. It is a passion in us that God can use.

For God wants that passion of ours. He wants to use it and to direct it. He has a good purpose for it. Possessing hatred is not a sin. It is how we use that hatred that is the sin.

Hatred used to consume evil is a glorious thing. Would that enough people besides Jews had been consumed with hatred toward Buchenwald, enough hatred to have destroyed it before it destroyed so many! Righteous indignation toward cruelty can stop that cruelty. To be aroused to stop the hand of the man who holds the whip requires a feeling of loathing so intense that cowardice is overcome.

But in order to possess that kind of hatred, that kind of loathing, a person has to possess something else in great quantity. For in order to hate evil, one must really love the good--love it, not just admire it, or be accustomed to it, or want it--one must love it.

To love people so much that one cannot bear to see them hurt;

To love justice so much that one cannot bear to see a man deprived of it;

To love learning so much that one cannot stand to see others lacking it;

To love the world so much one cannot bear to see it scarred by war and poverty and disease;

To love God so much that one cannot bear to hear his name abused without a shudder passing through one's body--

This is the only kind of love that can breed the right kind of hatred.

For there is another kind of love that makes hatred an evil, horrible emotion.

There is a love of security that makes it possible to hate people when they jeopardize it;

A love of sensuality that makes it possible to hate the person who will not satisfy it;

A love of status that makes it necessary to destroy those who threaten it;

A love of power that makes using it against others a satisfaction;

A love of self that makes preserving one's self the ultimate good, even if others are destroyed for that end.

This passion that is in us is such a volatile, dangerous, powerful force that there is only one person to whom we can trust it, and that is surely not ourselves. For this passion cannot be controlled by the intellect. Often the intelligent man will use his intellect to devise subtle and devious reasons for the misuse of his passion. He deceives himself as well as others.

The so-called good man cannot depend upon himself to make the right use of his passion. So often he will use it to justify his own particular interpretation of what is the will of God.

It is Jesus Christ to whom I must turn. But here again it is not simple. Jesus Christ is revealed to me through the Bible. The Bible is a book I must read and study before I can understand or interpret the events about which I should be passionate. Each event has to be scrutinized in its complete context before I make a rash judgment of hate. Jesus' words and acts must be clearly understood. Then once this is done, my feelings and my emotion should be given full sway to carry me along to the side of justice and love, to sweep me into the fight against evil, to pour into me the power to act for what is good.

But never to have any passion--never to love the good enough or to hate the evil enough to be aroused to action--this is a sad picture--a caricature of a man or woman--a wooden dummy--a pallid form--a lump of clay. In making man God made something that could be aroused by feelings so strong they could give him a glimpse of both heaven and hell. But the man who never lets them take possession of him will never glimpse either.

Love the good, hate the evil. Something should happen!

EVENING PRAYER

Night "steals" across the world.

"Steals," that is not a proper word either. Night doesn't steal. It brings something. It brings rest, quiet and peace as it softly hides the glare of the day. I turn off the light, shut off the radio and lie down. There! I open my eyes to the blackness.

There are no shadows, no grayness, no shapes, just dark. The noise of the world is muted, coming from a great distance.

Only God is here, the invisible, quiet, indestructible God who can fold me in his love, a love that heals, that blesses, that has fought the most diabolical forces in the world and by compassion, yearning and sacrifice has won the battle for me and all mankind.

"Jesus, who has done this for me, I close my eyes in thy love. Amen."

ON BEING ENVIOUS

Did you have a new brother or sister in your family when you were still a small child? Do you remember how it felt?

Your father walked in carrying the baby. He laid it on the bed. Your mother took you in her arms. She was home again. They let you hold the baby--for a minute.

Everything was great--until that moment a little later when your mother cradled that baby in her arms and looked at it the way mothers look at babies--the way she had always looked only at you.

Your heart gave a sudden lurch, you wanted to run out of the room. Nothing would ever be the same again.

For a moment, envy had gripped your soul in a powerful squeeze. There was someone who was now also the object of your mother's love and your father's pride.

Oh, you learned to live with it--you had to. But the envy didn't wholly disappear. All through your childhood you could remember incidents when you felt your brother or sister hadn't been punished as severely as you, or had been given more attention than you.

Envy was a virulent disease that would hit you more often than the common cold.

There was the teacher who was so excited by the creative spark in the theme of some other child--a theme that was not written nearly so neatly or perfectly as yours;

The time the coach picked another player to go on the trip even though that person's record was not better than yours;

The time your "crush" asked your best friend to the prom;

The times less effective preachers got called to larger congregations while you sat in your self-satisfied little parish;

The times other men said more effectively the things you had been thinking for a long time;

The times other people's children with less advantages than yours got awards and scholarships while yours muffed their chances.

So it goes, on and on, time after time.

Is there no way to inoculate oneself against envy?

There is.

Christians have known it for a long time. To avoid envy is an art. It is known as empathy. In order to empathize, a person must feel with the other person. To experience empathy, he enters into the other person's life as completely as he can.

When he hears a violinist playing beautifully, instead of wishing he could play like that, he lets the music of the violinist become his music as well. And the music carries him away on waves of sound.

There are the friends who have been to Europe or Pakistan or South America. Nothing gives them greater delight than to tell of their experiences and share their pictures. Instead of being bored by the whole thing or being jealous of the opportunity for travel, the Christian can see the wide world through their eyes. He can walk the streets and see the art treasures and feel his horizons enlarged.

Empathy is the ability to make everyone's experience one's own. That way life becomes so rich and so full that there is very little place left for envy.

Have you ever noticed in conversations that there are some people who do all the telling, who share their ideas and their experiences, but who never listen? Their lives are limited to what they do. If an event or pleasure does not happen to them personally, it might as well have never happened.

There are other people who ask questions, who seem interested in what others have to say, who delight in someone else's jokes and stories. They do this *not* merely to be polite, but because they have discovered the pleasurable experience of empathy, not just when they are at the theater or a concert, but every day with each person they meet.

In Christian terms this is known as the ability to lose oneself. The remarkable result of losing oneself in this way is that the little insignificant human being that one is becomes significant and enormous as one becomes a part of his friends, his community, his country and his culture.

It is really foolish and shortsighted to be envious. You have probably long ago outgrown such foolishness and have no need for this homily. But maybe some day when that long-ago-conquered vice suddenly pops up in the most unexpected place, with a sudden grab at your peace of mind, Jesus' words will come to you with added meaning, "He that loseth *his* life . . ."

EVENING PRAYER

I close my eyes and see nothing.

But that is not true. I can't really see nothing. My mind is like a moving film that goes on as long as I am awake. There are pictures going in and out of my consciousness--people I talked to today, the street as I walked down it, my house as I moved about in it.

I'll keep seeing things until I lose consciousness and I would be afraid to give up my consciousness if I could not pray.

"Eternal and almighty God, who art forever here as well as forever there, enter the inner parts of my mind to preserve the pictures that are of lasting value and to erase those pictures that have come from a slovenly application of my energy. In Jesus' name. Amen."

ON BEING STUPID

I am sure that many of you are saying, "At last she has picked a subject on which she is qualified to write."

It is true I have written on many topics, some of them profound ones from my limited viewpoint--a viewpoint circumscribed by my family, my church, my middle-class society and my particular kind of education.

I have not rebelled against these things. I have not stood outside and observed my background critically. I have not sought to enlarge my scope by indulging in experiences outside them. Rather, I have loved them and I have tended to resent, as well as not to understand, people who do not love them.

I realize this seems stupid to many people. It is only the woman of dull wit who is satisfied with her own husband, her own small house, her own little street, looking at the sun from the same window, seeing the moon rise from the same backyard, trotting to the same library, shopping in the same stores, worshiping in the same church, praying to the same God year in and year out.

The quick-witted person lets his life be filled with new sensations, experiments with revolutionary ideas, develops new concepts, wants to reach the far places of the earth. He is not satisfied to stand on tiptoe reaching toward the stars.

He wants to go there. He challenges each book, each sermon, each play, each speech he hears. He sees his family and his community in relation to many other things. His restless mind pulls him in many directions. He is never contented, never satisfied. He realizes there are many things he does not know, and he wants to know them.

He doesn't know the peace of the slower mind, the mind that hears the drone of rain on the roof and is glad there is a roof; the mind that feels the frigid snap of zero weather and is glad a wiser mind developed furnaces; the mind that repeats over and over again, "Lord, have mercy on me," to a God whose wisdom awes him but in whom he still trusts.

The reason he is contented with his little world is because this little world is never really the same to him even though it might look that way to the person whose experiences take him beyond his traditional environment.

Each day is not the same. The sun rises new to him each morning. The sky presents a new picture every day, different colors, different patterns, different cloud formations. His body never reacts in exactly the same way to various stimuli.

Sometimes he is soothed by a soft warm bed as he fades away into the nothingness of sleep. Other times his body tingles and bounces under a cold shower.

The people he sees never look quite the same to him because they never are the same. New cells are being made, old ones are dying. Each individual reacts to his particular environment in a different way.

Not being a mental giant, he never exhausts the books in the library. There are always authors he has never read. Every time he listens to his records he hears passages he has never really heard before.

I presume his world is limited because his mind is limited. It is always being satisfied with the newness of each day, the differences in familiar people, and the variety possible in the common practices of the day.

The unknown holds for him no fascination because he still feels unfamiliar with the known. His little problems are still big enough to be all he can handle. He only wishes he could handle them the way wiser persons appear to handle the world's problems.

No one likes to admit being stupid, and maybe stupid is not quite the proper word. Maybe small or little or of limited capacity would be a more gracious way of admitting that one is incapable of taking on any more problems or ideas or sensations.

It takes a huge mind with tremendous energy and unusual scope to do it. Apparently each age produces such people. Often we don't know who they are until they have been buried a long time.

There is only one person who claimed while he was alive to be the world's savior who after two thousand years is still claimed by many to be the world's savior.

Maybe to many this also appears to be stupid.

I cannot step outside myself and analyze this claim critically for it has been woven into the very fabric of my being from infancy. I cannot take that thread out of my fabric without unraveling the whole pattern. I really don't want to do that for I think that pattern is what makes me a whole person. The pattern without that thread would lose all its beauty and symmetry. I would be a meaningless jumble of threads and colors with nothing to give it form.

I can read and hear how other men evaluate that claim, but I read it all with a mind that has long been steeped in him so my reading is influenced by him.

He enters and fills the limited quality of my brain, so that to know God beyond him is not necessary for me.

I have to live with the fact that my world is small because I am small. But I have the strange feeling that even if my world were tremendous, he still could fill it.

EVENING PRAYER

How many times have I crawled into bed at night in my lifetime?

Thousand of times.

Have I ever gone to sleep without thinking of God?

I cannot remember any.

I have not always prayed. Sometimes I have been so bitter I have not prayed. Sometimes I have been so tired I have not prayed. Sometimes I have been so ill I have not prayed. Sometimes I have been so excited I have not prayed. Sometimes I have been so defiant I have not prayed.

But I have never gone to sleep unaware of God. He is the source of my life.

"Oh God, I pray thee to forgive the times I have neglected to commune with thee. I thank thee for the times when, through prayer, I have felt thy presence hovering about me. Be near me and those I love this night. In Jesus' name. Amen."

ON BEING PERFECT

He plunges his fork into chocolate cake. It is light and airy, but succulent and rich. "A perfect cake, dear," he tells his wife.

It is a perfect cake.

She opens the door. The sun dances into the hallway and the air rushes in, warm and fragrant with spring. "A perfect day, honey," she calls to her husband.

It is a perfect day.

A boy bursts into the house, flashing his report card in the air. "Guess, what, Mom, a perfect report card, all As," he shouts.

It is a perfect report card.

The nurse smiles as she walks quietly on rubber-soled feet into the waiting room. "A perfect baby boy," she says to the perspiring father.

But is it a perfect baby boy?

Oh, he has all his toes and fingers, and so forth. To his parents he looks perfect with his petal-soft skin, his soft, downy hair, and little round head.

But he is not perfect. He is not perfect because he is a human being. For everything human is imperfect. The seeds of imperfection are in that little child just as surely as the sun's warm rays blaze in continuous heat.

We do not like to believe this. We seem to have a craving for perfection.

I thought my mother and father were perfect--their judgment was infallible, their way of life flawless, and their faith as firm as the Rock of Gibraltar. They were very good parents, and they were the first to try to discourage my thoughts about their perfection. They knew that when I found out that they were not perfect, it was going to be a blow. It was.

I had teachers I thought were perfect. I read characteristics into them that were not there. They were often good teachers, but they had human flaws. I could never quite accept that, and I had my disappointments.

I had heroes and heroines among the great folk of my day. I wove fantastic tales around them that were not true. They were human and they fell flat and smashed into many pieces from the lofty pedestal on which I placed them.

Part of me was always crushed when I found these human flaws.

There were other human things which I thought were perfect that were not, because they were human.

I thought the college I attended was perfect. I didn't see or hear certain things that went on because I had decided that this was the most perfect institution of learning there was. But it was not and it is still hard for me to admit that it continues not to be everything I would like it to be

I thought the Lutheran Church was perfect. Then I found that it was plagued with the same kind of political maneuvering, unwieldy structure and reluctant reform that is found in every other democratic institution.

I thought the Bible was a perfect book without flaw, with each word the perfect one to describe the perfect thought. I was really shattered when I was exposed to a thorough study of the Bible, the divine Word written by human beings who could not even be perfect when they wrote this document.

I thought that at least my faith in Jesus Christ was perfect until that little craft was put out to sea. How it shuddered when the waves began to get high! How it filled with the water of despair when the storms blew! At one point it almost sank, but though it still flounders once in awhile, I have hopes it will make it to that other shore.

This does not deny the fact that Jesus is perfect or that God is perfect. But my understanding of him and my love of him are both imperfect. My judgment is not flawless. My love is not flawless. My faith is not flawless.

I am imperfect. So are you.

We were born that way.

We have lots of company, though. Paul and Peter admit to the same thing. Augustine and Luther never felt they had attained perfection.

What is the good of realizing we are imperfect? Doesn't it take all the incentive out of trying? Why run the race when we know we can't win?

We run the race because it has already been won. This is a paradox, isn't it?

To train, to exercise, to run, to pant, to exhaust oneself in a race that is already won, amazing!

But as Christians that is exactly what we need to do. We need to train ourselves in the Christian faith, we need to exercise ourselves in the art of prayer, we need to run fast to meet the needs of our fellowmen, we need to pant in our effort to resist evil, and we need to exhaust ourselves in lives of devotion to the winner of the race, Jesus Christ.

For then--it is comforting to know that though we have not attained, He has.

It is challenging to know that though we race with all the powers of evil--collective and individual, we must somehow win--for He has.

It is reassuring to know that though we stumble and fall, that though others stumble and fall, we can always stop long enough to pick ourselves and each other up because the race has been won--and we have the time.

EVENING PRAYER

How much should I do? Should I really get this tired? So tired! I think most of the things I did were good things. But I sometimes wonder if it is good to do so much that I never have time to think.

I should step back once in awhile and view the things I do with some sense of perspective. Maybe, though, it is not the amount of time that is important for perspective, maybe it is the height from which I look.

And there is no height higher than God.

"Oh God, I step back for a few moments to view my life--to be thankful for its tasks, to be thankful for the coming night that can refresh me, and to put my life into thy hands that thou wouldst renew it with thy vigor and enthusiasm. In Jesus' name. Amen."

ON BEING PATIENT

I hate to be patient. I hate to wait for something.

When I think of patience, I think of some slow, placid creature sitting with her hands folded, an eternal smile on her face, a buxom bottom amply filling the seat of a rocking chair.

A slow brain, a plodding step, an absence of expression seem the offspring of patience.

But show me the person who laughs quickly, who walks swiftly, who looks eager and alert. Very often he is an impatient man. He wants things done immediately. He wants to move the next minute. He wants to grasp the situation and push it along through sheer force of his own will. He doesn't want to wait.

Yet this is not always good. Patience is a virtue. Virtues are to be practiced. Whether I have wanted to practice virtue or not, I have had to.

It took me 18 years to be full grown.

I didn't learn to read in one day, as I expected to.

I couldn't play a hymn until I had taken piano for a year. I was not Mozart.

I was 18 before I had that first date I had been anticipating for four long teen-age years.

I had to write reams of letters and plot endless scintillating conversations before he asked me to marry him.

I had to wait nine long months for that baby. Even then, she was in no hurry, though she has been ever since.

It took me years to recover from an illness, or rather to rearrange my life so the illness would no longer keep me inactive.

Why the need for all this patience? Why couldn't things happen as soon as I wanted them to? Why did I always have to wait? Why do I still have to wait?

This long, wearying process teaches me something, though I am reluctant to learn.

I cannot do things by myself. I have to rely on other people. My wanting something does not make it appear like magic. I need parents, teachers, shopkeepers, doctors, a husband, all kinds of people to help me make dreams come true.

I cannot get these things from these people without trying to be agreeable. I must be pleasant whether I want to be or not.

I learn that other people have often devised better ways of doing things than I would have. During my waiting periods, I have often had to read, and my mind has had a chance to feast on other thoughts than my own.

I have been forced to look in on myself while I waited. I have found a great empty well in me that nothing seems to fill - ambitions, accomplishments, dreams, work, friends, family, It's a waiting place, a hungry place, a yearning place.

It is a place I sometimes forget when I am busy with other things. But when I am forced to be patient, I see it there. I feel it.

I find myself looking into this empty, empty well. It has to be filled because it makes me feel all hollow inside. It makes me seem like a fragile shell.

Somewhere there must be water ready to rush into this hole to fill it with the sparkle, the cleanness, the purity, the substance of fresh cool water.

Haven't I read that Jesus is the water that can fill my emptiness?

Of course, I have--in the Bible, in hymns, in the sacraments. But I have discovered that there is only one way that he will give it to me. Jesus gives me the water in a cup from which it is hard to drink. It is his cup. Once I take that cup I commit myself to a way of life from which there is no turning back. When I drink from his cup, I must walk his way; otherwise the cup becomes empty.

Do I want my emptiness taken away? Do I want to be more than a hollow drum, an empty well, a fragile shell?

There is only one way.

He has been patient with me, not with the rocking chair kind of plodding patience, but with the waiting patience of a mother holding out her hands for her child's first step, balanced, ready, taut to catch him as he toddles toward her.

So Jesus waits for me and for you.

EVENING PRAYER

"Oh Lord our God, who alone makest us dwell in safety, refresh us, who are wearied from the labors of the day, with quiet sleep this night; and mercifully protect from harm all who put their trust in thee, that, lying down in peace to take our rest, we may fear no evil, but confidently give ourselves into thy holy keeping through Christ our Lord. Amen."

ON BEING INTEMPERATE

Do you ever get drunk? Horrors! Of course not.

You are temperate in all things, aren't you? Moderation is the great thing, not abstinence or drunkenness, but the happy medium, the great middle-of-the-road.

But I am an abstainer when it comes to drinking alcohol, not necessarily because I advocate temperance but because I think intemperance is not a thing to be despised. When a person is an advocate of intemperance, there are only certain causes he can promote because there are only certain things and certain times when one can be intemperate, and drinking is *not* one of them!

Where is it possible to be intemperate?

In my house I have a stereo. I don't have it set so that the sound of music will form a background of gentle humming as I do my work. I set it so high that the sound of great music penetrates every cell of my body. I can't think. Every thought is drowned out.

I abandon myself completely to the sound and rhythm. I become drunk with music. What delicious abandon! There are no bad aftereffects. Rather, I feel as if I have been soaring like a bird, freed for a time from my earth-bound existence.

Or take the matter of kissing. I never kiss my husband in public nor do I expect him to kiss me. These polite little pecks are much too temperate. When I am kissed, I want to be kissed hard and to be hugged vigorously. Naturally, this restrains my kissing to only one person. But I'd rather abstain generally and really enjoy it specifically.

Oftentimes in our house and in our neighborhood we have discussions. I like to be able to say whatever pops into my mind without being misunderstood. I like to say it vigorously and I like to have others do the same. I don't like the feeling that I must weigh every word for fear that someone might be offended.

I have always felt that if a person's general attitude toward his friends is that of loyalty and good will, he should be able to speak his mind without being misinterpreted. I operate on the principle that it frees me to be completely honest and unaffected with no curbs on my speech. (You are right, I have unusually good neighbors!)

I also go to church with the idea that I can abandon myself to the worship experience. I love to sing hymns. It is really the only time I enjoy singing. So I sing loudly and gustily. One of my children frequently nudges me saying, "Do you have to sing so loudly?"

I have the feeling that being a Christian demands a certain amount of intemperance. I cannot be temperate in matters of faith and love. I have to abandon myself. I have to feel as free about my faith as I do about music or kissing or speaking or singing.

What did Jesus say? "Forgive thy brother seventy times seven." What intemperance in forgiveness!

"Love the Lord thy God with all thy mind, thy heart and thy soul." What intemperance in loving!

"When a man asks for a coat, give him two." What intemperance in giving!

"If a man hits you on one cheek, turn the other also." What intemperance in humiliation!

Christ does not give me little sips of love or forgiveness in tiny liquor glasses. He gives me great flagons full, from which I can gulp huge quantities. There is no moderation.

The intemperance about the Christian way of life is repugnant to many people. Moderation seems much more sensible, prudent, expedient. People like to do things properly and with decorum - well-run organizations, pleasant parties, quiet discussions, smooth conventions, well-groomed congregations.

But how can I fit Jesus into this way of life? Goodness knows I have tried--in my more temperate days. But he won't stay there. He doesn't belong there at all. He didn't when he lived on earth, and he doesn't now.

There are no limits. Jesus requires the abandoning of our little set of sensible rules of behavior. No rules are required for the kind of thing Jesus advocates.

It is only when we want to live within the structure of man-made society that the law must lay its heavy hand upon us.

In our society often the only reason we don't speed in our car is because me might be caught and have to pay a fine. Under Christ the only reason we wouldn't speed is because we might endanger other lives.

In our society often the only reason we pay our income tax is because there is a penalty if we don't. Under Christ we pay it because it is a means whereby people may be served through the function of the state.

It is curious the effect this kind of interpretation has. Freedom is no longer something about which one writes patriotic orations. This freedom comes not from doing exactly as one wishes. It comes from having been given wings by Jesus Christ to soar beyond human restrictions.

Christ tried hard when he was here to show men the way to shake off earth's musty ideas. He is still trying.

But his intemperance still shocks people. Sometimes I think they would almost prefer the other kind of intemperance, the kind we usually associate with that word. He can show contempt and disgust for that kind.

But with Jesus, what are we going to do with his kind of intemperance?

EVENING PRAYER

"Oh God, who hast drawn over weary day the restful veil of night, wrap our consciences in heavenly peace. Lift from our hands our tasks, and all through the night bear in thy bosom the full weight of our burdens and sorrow, that in untroubled slumber we may press our weakness close to thy strength and win new power for the morrow's duty from thee, who givest thy beloved sleep. Amen."

ON BEING TIRED

I wish I weren't so tired. Maybe you, too, sometimes feel as if a heavy blanket were lying across your shoulders, as if your legs weren't going to make that top stair, as if your eyes couldn't possibly stay open long enough to finish that page. Maybe you, too, are aware that your tiredness doesn't come from walking along a sandy beach or climbing mountains. It doesn't come from chasing children or baking bread.

It is a tiredness that comes from trying to decide who is right in government, in society, in the church. It is a tiredness about always being on the defensive when talking about faith in God, morality in sex, honesty in government.

Would you get so tired if you didn't care about right and wrong, about mercy and justice, about love and hate? Would you get so tired if you did not feel guilty of deceiving God, of despising people or belittling your heritage?

Perhaps it would be better if, like the flower, you turned your head toward the sun, indifferent to the other flowers around you. You would be more beautiful as a flower. Perhaps it would be better if, like a cat, you killed for your food, indifferent to the rightness or wrongness. You would be more relaxed. Perhaps it would be better if, like the shell on the seashore, you flowed with the tide, indifferent to emotional tensions. You would be more durable as a shell.

But for me, I'd rather be tired.

EVENING PRAYER

"Oh Lord, who hast pity for all our weakness, put from us worry and all misgiving, that having done our best while it was day, we may, when night cometh, commit ourselves, our tasks and all love into thy keeping, through Jesus Christ our Savior. Amen."